Ashwater's
Second Fulham Scrapbook

GW00585817

Reg Matthewson 1939–2016

Ashwater's
Second Fulham Scrapbook

Ken Coton and Martin Plumb

ASHWATER
PRESS

Books on Fulham Football Club published by Ashwater Press:

FULHAM'S GOLDEN YEARS
FULHAM – THE TEAM 1903–1995
FULHAM'S GOING UP!
THE COTTAGERS' JOURNALS
FOLLOWING THE FULHAM
FULHAM PHOTOS
PANDORA'S FULHAMISH BOX
FOLLOWING THE FULHAM INTO EUROPE
FOLLOWING THE FULHAM AROUND THE GROUNDS
A FULHAMISH COMING OF AGE
TALES FROM THE RIVERBANK – SEASONS 1965–66 AND 1966–67
TALES FROM THE RIVERBANK – SEASONS 1967–68 AND 1968–69
JOHNNY HAYNES – THE MAESTRO
FOLLOWING THE FULHAM – THE PREMIERSHIP YEARS
THE MICKY ADAMS PROMOTION SEASON – 1996–97
WHEN FULHAM WENT TO WEMBLEY
TALES FROM THE RIVERBANK – SEASONS 1969–70 AND 1970–71
FULHAM STRIKERS
FULHAM PHOTOS — VOLUME TWO
ASHWATER'S FULHAM SCRAPBOOK

Designed and published by
Ashwater Press
68 Tranmere Road, Whitton, Twickenham, Middlesex, TW2 7JB
www.ashwaterpress.co.uk.

Printed and bound by Henry Ling, Dorchester, England

ISBN 978-0-9927119-5-5

WELCOME TO a second scrapbook of Fulham stuff (as some supporters might call it), a dazzling cornucopia of all things Fulham (as we would like to call it).

Our more mature readers may remember a programme on the wireless called Semprini Serenade, where Mr Semprini played many a melodic tune on the piano. He introduced his programme with the softly-spoken words: "Old ones, new ones, loved ones, neglected ones." Those words fit this book very nicely, thank you.

In addition to delving into Ken's archive for pictures and delving into Martin's mind for facts both ordinary and extraordinary, we have been delighted to use material sent in from supporters far and wide, and we thank them heartily. Their pictures have certainly raised the tone of the book.

So, in here you will find old pictures (oh, no, I've seen that picture a hundred times before), new pictures (well, I never), loved ones (well, I've seen it before, but it's still quite nice) and neglected ones (oops, I can see why it was neglected).

We thank all Ashwater friends, supporters and customers for their continued support of this little corner of Whitton that is forever Fulham. Thanks also to the Fulham club for their help in making the first scrapbook a sell-out.

Fulham FC is special to us; we love our club, and in these pages you may catch glimpses of the trials and tribulations, as well as the glories and successes, that it has been through, dragging us along with it.

Keep going, Fulham; or in more technical terms: 'Come on, you Whites!'

Ken Coton and Martin Plumb, Ashwater Press, Whitton, October 2016

THANKS

*Our thanks to the many supporters and friends who have helped with pictures and words for this book, including Brian Broughton, Darren Brown, Paul Cooper, Phil Cowan, Javier Garcia, June Gilbert, Maureen Grimwood, Yvonne Haines, Jon Hall, Robert Heath, Peter Heffernan, Derek Hicks, Ed Holford, David Instone, Patrick Mascall, Brian Nichols, Kevin O'Callaghan, Mick Petrovic, Joanna Plumb, Gillian Ray (via Neil Springate), Mick Roots, Mark Sheldrake, John Stubbs, David Tachon, Sheila Thomson, Dave Wilson, Peter Woodman
– and our apologies to anyone we've missed.*

Special thanks to Robert Fennell for his proofreading and editorial expertise.

The boardroom in the Riverside Stand in the 1970s, ready for action.

Left: Talking of action, let's get a Les Strong picture out of the way right now – here he is clashing with Huddersfield defenders.

Below: Three budding Fulham fans pose on the Cottage steps; they're hanging on to the handrail, as they know it's going to be a bumpy ride supporting their favourite club.

Fulham lose a grim struggle

INJURED COHEN MISSES SECOND-HALF

FULHAM 0, LEICESTER 1

HAROLD PALMER: Craven Cottage, Saturday

That relegation bogey pressed hard on Fulham here as they struggled grimly with a depleted team to cancel the lead visitors Leiceste

A bare tree complements bare fortunes for the Whites. In a sea of mud and sand, and without leading scorer Allan Clarke, Fulham are beaten 0–1 at home by a mediocre Leicester side in January 1968. Manager Vic Buckingham was 'relieved of his duties' a few days afterwards with Fulham anchored at the bottom of the table.

Below: a photocall from the same era, with Johnny Haynes showing the photographers just how it's done. At left in the background is our own Ken Coton, doing his Alfred Hitchcock impersonation, and for once not looking grumpy.

All eyes are on a ball that's not in the picture during a Bristol Rovers attack in April 1982, on the way to Fulham's well deserved promotion that season. Dean Coney (second Fulham player from the right) is back helping out the defence. The other Fulham players are Tony Gale, Jeff Hopkins and Roger Brown. Fulham won this one easily by 4–2.
  As an aside, the Rovers side that day contained three players with the surname Williams and there was another in the squad – might have made team selection a little complicated!

Opposite page: *Sean O'Driscoll returns to the Midlands area (he joined Fulham from Alvechurch) to slide home Fulham's goal past the advancing keeper in the 1–1 draw at Walsall in the same month as the Rovers picture above. This was at Fellows Park and just a few years later, Walsall would 'move on' to the Bescot Stadium.*
  The old stand shown in the picture promotes the local radio station where Jasper Carrott, among others, took his first steps to fame. The station name, BRMB, was not an acronym. The original company, Birmingham Broadcasting Ltd, wanted something that combined a US-style call sign with the company name, so Birmingham (BRM) was combined with broadcasting (B), making BRMB – as simple as that.

Here is a November 1967 view of trees and houses at Newcastle before St James's Park became a concrete stadium. Les Barrett has another effort saved by the advancing keeper Marshall. Despite dominating the game and taking an early lead, Fulham eventually lost 1–2, going down to a controversial late winner when Ian Seymour was virtually knocked out by a flying elbow.

Right: George Noyce watches Ronnie Goodlass sign for Fulham from Den Haag. The former Everton player was with Fulham for just half a season in 1980–81, before moving on to Scunthorpe. He scored twice, both times away from home. Ronnie is signing with the right hand, the left arm obscured. He had lost his left hand in an equipment accident, so was one of the earliest 'disabled' players competing in League football.

This picture shows Arthur Rowley (right) at Shrewsbury Town. Rowley played briefly for Fulham after the war where he scored freely and will be remembered mostly as the player who scored both goals in a 2–0 win over West Ham that gave us the 1948 Second Division championship and promotion for the first time to the top flight. He left for Leicester City where his record breaking scoring continued. Finally he moved to Shrewsbury Town where he also became their record goalscorer. He retired at 37 to become manager in 1965. He moved on in 1968 and is here pictured handing over the reins to a younger man, Harry Gregg, the former Manchester United goalkeeper and survivor of the Munich disaster. Rowley holds the record for the most goals in the history of English league football, scoring 434 from 619 league games.

Fulham were sponsored by Teleconnect in 1990–91; although the players seem happy enough in this squad picture, one does wonder whatever happened to Teleconnect...

Left: The game at Millwall in January 1974 was the first ever first-class match to be played on a Sunday, though Sunday-like behaviour seemed lacking as a linesman keeps a Millwall player away from our poor little Jimmy Conway.

Right: It's a goal; it's a hug.

Below: a great picture of an unknown celebrity surrounded by Johnny Haynes, Bill Dodgin, Jimmy Hill and Dave Sexton. However, the occasion is unidentified, as are the badges on the shirts.

Crowded out by Hereford defenders, John Mitchell in change strip fails to connect fully with a cross in March 1977 at Edgar Street. A winless run of ten matches had seen Fulham sliding quickly towards relegation from the Second Division. However, the 0–1 defeat here at Hereford United proved to be a watershed match and Fulham got it together afterwards, losing just two of the next eleven, and slowly clawing themselves to safety.

Below: Mary Doughty, the Supporters' Club superstar, is pictured in 1970 exchanging a chat with Fulham centre half Dave Roberts protecting himself from the wind. Don't let that bar between them fool you! In those days, players and supporters mixed freely. Roberts had the misfortune of being a member of a poorish Fulham side and as usual they gave him away for a pittance after just a handful of games, only to see him play 300 games for Oxford, Hull and Cardiff, winning seventeen international caps for Wales in the process.

During a poor time for British football and to stop increasing violence and pitch invasions in the late 70s and early 80s, metal fencing was placed around the perimeter of grounds to mitigate such threats. Here in March 1982 at the Cottage, the Burnley keeper is given treatment during a 1–1 draw. Despite the glances towards the crowd, there was no way that such an injury could have been caused by a missile from the respectful Fulham faithful.

Below: Two goals down at Sheffield United in April 1968 with just twenty minutes remaining, Fulham scored three goals in eleven minutes to secure their first victory at Bramall Lane in thirteen visits. The third, victory-clinching goal was scored by Joe Gilroy who latched on to a John Ryan pass. In the picture, Gilroy salutes his goal and the end of a jinx.

THE LES BARRETT FAN CLUB

YES ' THERE IS AN
OFFICIAL
LES BARRETT
FAN CLUB

REGULAR NEWSHEET
PHOTOGRAPHS
COMPETITIONS

JOIN

By sending 3/- with your name
and address to :-

Les Barrett Fan Club,
Fulham Football Club,
Stevenage Road,
LONDON SW 6

Les Barrett Fan Club,
Craven Cottage,
London SW 6

Dear Sir, I wish to become a Member of your Fan
Club, and I enclose 3/- for my membership

Signed ....

Name & Address ....

OUTSIDE LEFT
LES BARRATT

Here's Les Barrett, our favourite winger from the 60s and 70s. At top right that's Les and brother Paul recording their hit single 'Julie Brown loves Captain Cook'; at top right the lads show off their Trend Trackers, devices designed to promote fitness.

The fan club was started in 1967 as Les's prominence in football rose. As can be clearly seen, no Word documents in those days! Subscription would be £2.50 today – perfectly reasonable!

An early collector's card managed to mis-spell his name.

The action picture shows Les up against the late great Harry Cripps of Millwall in 1969. Fulham won the London derby that day, and yes, Les got the first goal.

Fondly remembered for his fine dashing football, at right Les flaunts his, er, fine physique.

And here's Les in action at Villa in March 1966. At least he is moving – the other Fulham players in the picture seem to be just hanging around.

Below: a goal from the same match in which Les scored in the 5–2 victory. But this was not his goal; instead we feature one of the two that Steve Earle (number 7) scored that afternoon.

An FA Cup replay in February 1968. On a misty night, a massive crowd of almost 44,000 cram into Fratton Park to see the fourth-round tie against First Division Fulham. Fulham fight all the way and are undone by Second Division Portsmouth via a tap-in from Mike Trebilcock (whose two goals had won the FA Cup for Everton two years before). Fulham manage to hit the bar and have several other second-half near misses.

In the picture Fulham seem to have a good penalty shout as the defender appears to go through Allan Clarke whose legs are unceremoniously taken away, but is it a clean sliding tackle with the momentum taking the man? Would today's referees allow that? No penalty is awarded, and for the sixth year running Fulham fail to progress beyond the fourth round of the cup.

The date is May 1971 and it's all smiles from the crowd as young captain Barry Lloyd leads out his Fulham team for the season's final home match against Preston North End. Promotion for the Cottagers from Division Three had been achieved away at Bradford City in midweek, and a single point against the men from Deepdale would give Fulham the championship.

Alas it's a leg-weary deflating performance against a rugged and determined Preston who would become champions with a victory against us and a win in their last remaining match. Fulham give their all, but the jaded players are half a yard behind Preston. Here, below, goalkeeper Kelly makes a routine collect from another cross as Earle and Johnston wait for a possible error. In a game few will wish to remember, the Whites fail to collect the point they need and lose 0–1. Fulham's nemesis Heppolette, who scored Preston's goal, is visible through the net – grrrrr!

Fans join in celebrations at Fulham Town Hall following the Cottagers' championship of Division One in 2001.

With captain Chris Coleman in the top picture are Mark Sheldrake (at right) and his brother, Paul.

Also pictured here are goalkeeper Maik Taylor and manager Jean Tigana.

Above: Nick Cusack in action during a fine 4–1 win for the Cottagers at Cardiff in March 1996.

Left: Jamie Smith scores his only goal for Fulham just before half time at Walsall in May 1999, to bring the score to 1–1. Both Walsall and Fulham were already promoted, with Fulham already champions, and the match turned out to be a free-flowing exciting encounter. Walsall went ahead for a second time ten minutes from the end, only for Fulham to secure a well-deserved draw with a cracking shot from Steve Hayward (below) in the last two minutes.

It seems like yesterday, but it was over 15 years ago. Just take a look at the players from both sides listed on the team sheet that afternoon in September 2001 and feast on the quality of both squads.

There were two firsts that day; one was record signing Steve Marlet appearing for the first time as a Fulham substitute. Here he forces David Seaman into a decent save. The ball IS in the picture (which pleased photographer Coton) but is hard to spot at first glance.

Below, our goal that day – and a fine one too. It's the other first in the match as it was Steed Malbranque's first goal for the club.

Arsenal grabbed the spoils on this occasion with a 3–1 victory, but it was part of a learning curve for the promoted Whites.

Where did fifteen years go!

FULHAM FOOTBALL CLUB
V
ARSENAL FOOTBALL CLUB
15TH SEPTEMBER 2001

EDWIN VAN DER SAR	1		1	DAVID SEAMAN
STEVE FINNAN	2		3	ASHLEY COLE
RUFUS BREVETT	3		4	PATRICK VIEIRA (Capt)
ANDY MELVILLE (Capt)	4		5	MARTIN KEOWN
KIT SYMONS	6		7	RUBERT PIRES
JOHN COLLINS	10		8	FREDERICK LJUNGBERG
STEED MALBRANQUE	14		9	FRANCIS JEFFERS
SYLVAIN LEGWINSKI	18		12	GWINSKI LAUREN
LOUIS SAHA	20		14	THEIRY HENRY
SEAN DAVIS	23		15	RAY PARLOUR
LUIS BOA MORTE	22		23	SOL CAMPBELL
			10	DENNIS BERGKAMP
MAIK TAYLOR	12		11	SYLVAN WILTORD
LEE CLARK	8		16	GIOVANI BRONCKHURST
STEVE MARLET	9		18	GILLES GRIMANDI
BARRY HAYLES	15		24	RICHARD WRIGHT
ABDESLAM OUADDOU	25			

Referee	Mr A Wiley
Assistant Referee	Mr R Burton
Assistant Referee	Mr K Woolmer
4th Official	Mr B Knight

Talking of famous players, just take a look at the Swansea team (right) that played at Craven Cottage on Boxing Day 1955 – not only the two Allchurch brothers, Ivor and Len, but also Mel Charles, younger brother of the great John Charles, as well as Cliff Jones, later to join Fulham, and Terry Medwin, later to become a Fulham coach.

The match was a comfortable win for the Cottagers, by four goals to one, with Haynes grabbing a couple, including a penalty. The reverse fixture took place the following day (being the third league match in four days!) and of course Fulham lost, as Swansea scored two goals without reply.

FULHAM

White Shirts, Black Knickers.

R	L

BLACK

2 WILSON   3 LAWLER

4 SMITH   5 GREENWOOD   6 LOWE, E.

8 HILL   10 HAYNES

7 BARTON   9 JEZZARD   11 CHAMBERLAIN

Referee—
Mr. F. COWEN
(Manchester)

Linesmen—
Mr. P. STRATTEN
(Yellow Flag)
Mr. C. PEGG
(Red Flag)

11 JONES, C.   9 MEDWIN   7 ALLCHURCH, L.

10 ALLCHURCH, I.   8 GRIFFITHS

6 JONES, B.   5 CHARLES   4 HENNINGS

3 THOMAS   2 WILLIS

L	R

KING

SWANSEA TOWN

Champions

FULHAM FC NATIONWIDE FIRST DIVISION CHAMPIONS 2001-01

The Sport friday

BRITAIN'S ONLY SPORTS NEWSPAPER ● MAY 30 1997

PULL OUT

Harrods
FOOTBALL CLUB

AL FAYED SPENDS £30m AS TOP PEOPLE'S STORE SNAPS UP SOCCER BARGAIN AT FULHAM

REPORT AND ANALYSIS: PAGE 3

16 PAGES

TENNIS
Venus crashes to Earth in Paris during early exit on French clay
Page 16

WIN £5,000

END OF THE GAME

SHOCK waves of anger and disbelief swept through Fulham's community this week with the news its football club is to be merged with QPR.

Outbursts of fury came from all sides, with Fulham's MP Nick Raynsford taking the front seat in a blistering attack on the new owners of Craven Cottage, writes Kate Bresler.

Mr Raynsford has called on Fulham Football Club's chairman, David Bulstrode, to keep his pledge that football will continue to be played at Craven Cottage for at least two more years.

And he has warned: "If he doesn't give me that then I have to say it is one of the most appalling examples of cynicism and duplicity I have ever come across.

On Monday Mr Bulstrode made the shock announcement that Fulham was merging with QPR and

moving to the Loftus Road grounds in the north of the borough.

Craven Cottage will now be developed for private housing.

He said: "When I said we'd stay at the Cottage for at least three years I hadn't foreseen how the gates have gone down and I didn't know that QPR would become available."

Over the past three years Fulham has lurched from one crisis to another.

Three applications to develop the Bishops Park end of the grounds have been turned down by Hammersmith and Fulham's planning chiefs, both Tory and Labour.

Roz Denny of Bishops Park Co-ordinating Group, which has led local residents bid to stop any over-development of the site, said: "We are very apprehensive about the future of the ground and will be watching matters very closely. We are obviously very sorry about Fulham Football Club and were happy for them to stay."

Mr Raynsford said: "I believe people in Fulham and across the country will be deeply shocked. Fulham FC has a long, proud tradition and is greatly loved in Fulham.

"There are many of us who will be fighting tooth and nail to stop the club from being kicked around by people whose interests are in property developing.

"I will be raising the matter in the House of Commons at the earliest possible moment and I shall be giving my absolute wholehearted support to saving Fulham Football Club," he added.

Council leader councillor Gordon Prentice said he was as shocked as the many thousands of fans.

"There are millions of pounds at stake here and Mr Bulstrode has acted in totally bad faith. We were waiting for the club to be resurrected as he promised, but what we have got is property speculation."

'Send No White Lilies' — the history of Fulham Football Club in pictures — page 26.

> 'When I said we'd stay at the Cottage for at least three years, I hadn't foreseen how the gates have gone down and that QPR would become available'
> — DAVID BULSTRODE

> 'I will be raising the matter in the House of Commons at the earliest possible moment and giving my wholehearted support to saving Fulham Football Club'
> — NICK RAYNSFORD, MP

The highs and the lows of supporting Fulham Football Club: always colourful, always a roller-coaster – and more often than not a challenge! Thanks to Paul Cooper for the three colour newspaper pictures.

HISTORY

Roy salutes his final heroes

FULHAM 2 HAMBURG 1

By PAUL JIGGINS

ROY HODGSON hailed his history makers after Fulham reached the Europa League final.

Simon Davies and Zoltan Gera dragged the Cottagers back from a goal down. Boss Hodgson said: "We

made a major piece of history here. The atmosphere is something we will remember for a long time and we're delighted to be in the final.

"Many teams might have crumbled after their

www.thesun.co.uk/sport

A £6m investment — Full Story — Page 97

SOLD

CRAVEN COTTAGE SOLD

Fulham Football Club have been forced to admit that the ownership of the Craven Cottage site has been transferred from Fulham Stadium Limited to Fulham River Projects Limited. Fulham River Projects is a finance and development company set up to redevelop the Craven Cottage site. The sole director of the company is a senior partner at Forsters, a leading property law firm. The company was set up on 18 September 2002 - even though until late December the Club was saying that rebuilding Craven Cottage was the priority, and the Chairman claimed it was "99% certain" that we would return. So why was Fulham River Projects set up ?

It seems that Fulham Football Club have no intention of ever re-building Craven Cottage as a football stadium, despite statements to the contrary, and with no alternative options identified, the future of the Club is in doubt. IT IS TIME FOR THE TRUTH FROM MOHAMMED AL FAYED - where will Fulham Football Club play

BACK TO THE COTTAGE PUBLIC MEETING
7.30 PM Thursday 30th January 2003 at Hammersmith Town Hall

Back to the Cottage is an independent Fulham fans' group devoted solely to ensuring the return of Fulham FC to its traditional riverside home. For more info www.backtothecottage.com

Anger at club merger plan

By NEIL BARNETT

Fulham are dead. Long live Rangers

At 5.30 pm on Monday, Fulham chairman David Bulstrode handed out a statement, with Queens Park Rangers chairman Jim Gregory seated at his side, announcing the merger of the two clubs with himself in charge. The move takes place at the end of the season.

QPR manager Jim Smith and chief executive Dennis Signy had been informed 15 minutes earlier. Fulham player manager Ray Lewington, returning after his cartilage operation and ironically playing and scoring for the reserves in their 2-1 afternoon win over QPR Reserves was told after the game. Smith manages the new club.

Of Lewington, Bulstrode said: "We will be discussing his position in terms of the new club." Smith, present at the press conference,

and move to Wembley."

Bulstrode said he saw no problem of preserving Fulham as an ongoing entity. However, with the low support they've suffered from of late he clearly felt little accountability in that area.

"When I said we'd stay at The Cottage for at least three years I hadn't foreseen how the gates have gone. And I didn't know that QPR would become available."

Reaction from QPR supporters was not

in the bottom four now. Where does it all go? Once they've got the club there why keep it? It's a prime site for the BBC."

Most of Fulham's 25 administrative posts are likely to go and only a handful of players can expect a new career with the new club. QPR will get Paul Parker, whom they tried to buy at the beginning of the season, some good youngsters, a slightly new name, and of course a new board of directors. But in reality,

Fulham manager Malcolm Macdonald chats with Harold Genders on the pitch in 1980. Genders had played rugby league for Rochdale Hornets, Widnes and Blackpool Borough before retiring in 1958. He became a director of Warrington RLFC in the mid-1970s. He wanted to 'spread the gospel' of the sport he loved into the south, and in 1980 approached chairman Ernie Clay. Clay agreed with the 'Fulham idea' and Fulham applied for membership of the RFL. When the application was accepted, Genders resigned his directorship at Warrington, and became Fulham's rugby league managing director. His role was primarily player recruitment, and he built a wonderful team for that memorable first promotion season at Fulham in 1980–81. Macdonald was one of the first directors of the rugby league club.

Right: a wooden board from the Sixties showing Fulham's early fund-raising with the 'improvement society'. There was a draw every day during the week with three lucky winners. The numbers were placed on the board probably with chalk, but just how the winners were informed is unknown. The board was used around 1960–65; the first prize of £15 is worth about £300 today.

For the commuter and the man about town, the must-have accessory was a Fulham lunch box. It also contained a plastic drinks flask adorned with the club crest, ideal for putting on display on the office desk.

Right: During the Fifties, the only pennant usually seen on a boy's push bike (BSA or Raleigh with 3 Sturmey Archer gears, anyone?) was a green felt 'cycling proficiency test' prize. Some thought that it was a bit posh or embarrassing to stick on your handlebars, so yearned for something a little more 'cool'. What better than a Fulham FC pennant! Supporter Peter Woodman had this on his bike sixty years ago, given to him by his Dad after being taken to his first Fulham game. It still looks cool.

Intertoto cup-winning night at Loftus Road in August 2002. Fulham chairman Mohamed Al Fayed poses with manager Tigana and the cup. The players stand around seemingly stunned. Is that the only cup Fulham have ever won?

At right in the picture (and second from top) is David Hamilton, ready to add his cultured tones to the moment, whilst at bottom centre of the picture, in the grey hat, is photographer Ken Coton, working hard.

Below: a trip to Berlin in the UEFA Europa League, the competition that followed the Intertoto victory. Here fans are snapped in front of the Brandenburg Gate, among them Ashwater friends Derek Jeffery on the left and the late Peter Thomson on the right.

A Steed Malbranque grassless corner at Loftus Road in February 2003 against Burnley in the fifth round of the FA Cup. Steed scored Fulham's goal that day in a match where Burnley somehow escaped with an undeserved draw. As for the replay...well, we Fulham fans know all about our visits to Turf Moor. (We lost, of course.)

The changing face of photographers. Above left are modern photographers (as seen on the previous spread) with their big lenses, automatic digital cameras and, for heaven's sake, computers. They can now check, edit and send off their pictures in a moment. In olden days it was more leisurely, and there was even time for a chat with a goalkeeper, above right.

The picture below captures a significant moment in the match against Bristol City in August 1978. No, not the throw-in, but the helmeted motor-bike rider. It's about twenty minutes into the match and he's come from Fleet Street to collect exposed film to be rushed back for developing and inclusion in later editions of the papers. Woe betide any photographer who hadn't been able to capture any action in those first twenty minutes! No doubt that was why he was at the end Fulham were attacking...

Pictured at left is a standard 'welcome to Fulham' photo snapped by the press on George Best's arrival at Craven Cottage.

Somehow our own photographer managed to get George on his own and snapped the sultry portrait above.

Did you have a talisman or mascot that you took to every Fulham match in the hope or belief that it would help the team to win? Peter Woodman carried with him the little figure pictured here; his mother dressed it in Fulham colours which she knitted herself. 'It still didn't help us win a proper cup...' bemoans Peter.

These two pages are an Ashwater tribute to our own George Cohen, hero of England's World Cup win in 1966. Pictured above is Ken Coton's view from the terraces of that disputed England goal – did it cross the line?

JULES RIMET CUP
WORLD CHAMPIONSHIP
ENGLAND 1966 JULY 11-30
WEMBLEY·EVERTON·SHEFFIELD·SUNDERLAND·ASTON VILLA· MANCHESTER·MIDDLESBROUGH·WHITE CITY

OFFICIAL SOUVENIR PROGRAMME

R. MOORE   R. WILSON   J. CHARLTON   J. ARMFIELD   T. PAINE   G. HURST

I. CALLAGHAN

M. PETERS

ENGLAND

22 Selected Players

1 Gordon Banks	12 Ronald Springett
2 George Cohen	13 Peter Bonetti
3 Ramon Wilson	14 James Armfield
4 Norbert Stiles	15 Gerald Byrne
5 John Charlton	16 Martin Peters
6 Robert Moore	17 Ronald Flowers
7 Alan Ball	18 Norman Hunter
8 James Greaves	19 Terence Paine
9 Robert Charlton	20 Ian Callaghan
10 Geoffrey Hurst	21 Roger Hunt
11 John Connelly	22 George Eastham

The names and numbers of the players taking part in each match will be announced over the public address system prior to the kick-off. This information should be inserted in the space provided on the relevant page for each game, covered between pages 44 and 55.

Les noms et les numéros des joueurs sélectionnés seront annoncés par moyen du haut-parleur avant le coup d'envoi de chaque match. Ces renseignements sont à ajouter à la page qui convient, c'est-à-dire entre la page 44 et la page 55.

Die Namen und Nummern der Spieler welche an jedem Spiel teilnehmen, werden per Lautsprecher vor dem Anstoss bekannt gegeben. Diese Angaben können an der hierfür für jedes Spiel vorgesehenen Stelle—Seiten 44 bis 55—eingetragen werden.

Los nombres y números de los jugadores que toman parte en cada partido serán anunciados por los altavoces antes del comienzo del partido. Esta información debe ser incluida en la casilla correspondiente en la página relativa a cada partido, incluida entre las páginas 44 y 55.

J. CONNELLY

N. HUNTER

G. COHEN

A. BALL

G. BYRNE

R. SPRINGETT

R. CHARLTON

P. BONETTI

R. HUNT   G. EASTHAM   J. GREAVES   N. STILES   G. BANKS   R. FLOWERS

29

Above: the aftermath of the goal opposite. German players at left in the picture accost the linesman; there are even a couple of excited photographers on the pitch. Cue for a Wolstenholme quote: "...and now Hurst, can he do it? He has done, yes! Yes! No! No! The linesman says, 'No.' The linesman says, 'No.' ...it's a goal!"

Left: at last, a statue of George, recently unveiled at the Cottage. Below: the Riverside Stand and the entrance to George's hospitality suite. Inset: one-club man George helping out with a pitchside presentation. We of Fulham are proud to have seen and known George, a genuinely nice, normal guy; and remember – England only win the World Cup when there's a Fulham player in the team...

A tribute to Stan Brown – Mr Reliable, a one-club man for fifteen years, with just short of 400 appearances. In the days of logically numbered shirts, Stan Brown wore every outfield shirt from 2 to 11 with equal effectiveness. If he had been taller he would have probably played in goal too. Never one for the limelight, he swept up all over the pitch for Fulham with tireless energy, letting the gifted players put the finishing touches to his hard work. An enthusiast for football he was often the first to training even though he came all the way in from Sussex to train. As skipper Haynes said, 'You never notice him, until you need him.' After league football, Stan continued playing at a high level in Sussex until he was over forty.

Left: captains. Proud Stan posing on the Cottage pitch and, inset, leading out the East Sussex schoolboys.

Above: pictures of one of Stan's goals against Blackburn in August 1965. Despite not being the tallest player in the world, Stan scored a number of his career goals (19) with his head, and they were often spectacular. Here he runs twenty-five yards to connect with a cross and plant a firm header into the net.

Below: Tea and sandwiches, anyone? Stan with colleagues John Dempsey and Steve Earle.

Below right: Stan collected a whole array of badges throughout his career.

A real car-crash of a picture. Tony Mahoney (in the air), Peter Marinello and Gordon Davies all try to get the better of a Luton Town defence in September 1979, but everyone seems to have missed the ball. In the end all Fulham had to show for their efforts that afternoon was a Kevin Lock penalty – and their first home defeat of the season. Luton won 1–3 and by the end of the season Fulham were relegated to the Third Division.

Below: It's the final match of the 1998–99 season and Paul Moody drills home a penalty with the Preston goalkeeper guessing wrongly. Moody had come on as a second-half substitute and created Fulham history by becoming the only player ever to score a hat trick as a substitute. The fact that all three goals came in just a thirteen-minute spell makes the feat all the more remarkable. They were two headed goals with this penalty sandwiched in between. It's made even more unique (yes, Mr Editor, we know things can't really be more unique, but you know what we mean...) by the fact that it turned out to be Moody's last game in a Fulham shirt. They were also the only goals in the match.

FULHAM F.C. SUPPORTERS CLUB

"COTTAGE PIE"

MAY 1966

HEADQUARTERS

" THE GOLDEN LION "

FULHAM HIGH STREET, S.W.6.

PRESIDENT : J.H.BARRON, ESQ.

CHAIRMAN : S.C.R.HUGGETT, ESQ.

Below: the aftermath of Steve Earle's goal in the final two minutes that puts Fulham ahead for the first time (3–2) in the crucial relegation 'decider' match against Northampton Town in 1966. The joy on the Fulham faces is almost tangible, whilst the Northampton defender knows what it means for his team.

Earle's breakaway goal in injury time completed his hat trick and put the result beyond doubt. On the right is an early typewriter version of modern word-processed documents which appeared in the May 1966 edition of Cottage Pie. Here Mike Saich describes in detail the events of that nerve-wracking afternoon in April.

TRAVELLERS TALE
by Mike Saich

On reflection, there is really one away game one could write about – Northampton Town on April 23rd 1966. Who could possibly have foreseen on that August evening when Blackburn Rovers left the Cottage on the wrong end of a 5-2 hiding, that eight months later the status of Fulham F.C. would be decided on a county cricket ground in the Midlands. That, however, is what soccer is all about.

The position was quite clear – having been beaten at home 0-4 by Leicester City on the previous Monday, it was essential to win at Northampton to go above the Cobblers on goal average. Defeat would mean a four points lag with only three games to play – two of them away from home.

Interest in this match surpassed anything we in the Supporters Club have experienced outside the F.A. Cup Semi-Finals. In our promotion year we made history by chartering a special train for the Easter Monday league game at Sheffield Wednesday, but numerically, this was small beside the crowd at the Northampton County ground.

A record 15 coaches left Colehill Lane, two trains from St. Pancras were packed, and hundreds of fans made the journey up the M.1. by car, motor cycle or anything that would carry them the 70 odd miles. I made the trip by car, and it was very interesting to see the enormous number of both Fulham and Chelsea (playing their cup semi-final v. Sheffield Wednesday at Villa Park) supporters making their way to the Midlands. It was a pleasant trip lasting about two hours, and even 1½ hours before the kick off crowds were assembling and parking becoming difficult. It was the first time most of us had seen the Cobblers ground and, I think, we were surprised to see how well they packed in a record gate (24,523). The temporary terracing opposite the grandstand seemed full to bursting point, but all was well by the time 3.0 p.m. arrived.

Naturally with so much at stake, nerves were much in evidence on both sides, but we hoped that our greater experience would tell to our advantage as the game progressed. The vital first goal went to Northampton, but soon a superb Bobby Robson equaliser had our supporters behind the goal jumping for joy. A second goal to the home side before half time led us to wonder if we could pull something extra out after the interval. Greater determination and football skill gradually swung the game and a typical George Cohen right wing sprint led to a second leveller, this time by Steve Earle.

Both sides now, while not playing for a draw, appeared to be concentrating on not making mistakes, and a division of the points seemed inevitable with the score at 2-2 with less than two minutes to play. Then Steve Earle struck again – first heading in a Graham Leggatt pinpointed centre and finally running threequarters of the length of the field with only Graham Leggatt for company before rounding the goalkeeper and making the game safe. It was a fantastic goal to end a fantastic match.

Everyone was stunned – especially the home crowd – they knew the significance of that defeat – as did the happy thousands of Fulham fans who could hardly believe it had really happened. The rest is history now, by the following Saturday evening we were safe and Northampton were relegated to Division two. We wish them a speedy return and can certainly say that they gave us a match to remember for a long time to come. Let us hope that our players can continue to produce displays up to the standard seen during the past two months when next season comes around.

Les Barrett shows style and power as he torments Cardiff defenders in 1975.

Below: Burnley goalkeeper Adam Blacklaw collects cleanly watched by defender Alex Elder and England international forward Ray Pointer. Maurice Cook (at left) is out of the action and Brian O'Connell gets no joy. The game was in April 1963.

Bottom: It's late in the game against Workington in a League Cup replay on a foul and windy Monday night in October 1967. The Fourth Division side, having been two goals down, have somehow dragged themselves back to 2–2 by the hour mark and First Division Fulham are struggling. Fortunately Les Barrett scores a wonder solo goal and, with the Cumbrian side finally deflated, Allan Clarke then scores a 'real' hat trick (three consecutive goals) in the last twenty minutes to secure the win for the Cottagers; the hat trick goal is shown in the picture. It was four goals on the night for Clarke, soon to become an international player.

This looks like a case for goal-line technology, but in fact the ball is on the way in. Not that it did much good. It's January 1976 and, after our fantastic exploits in the FA Cup the previous season, Fulham are hoping for something of a repeat; what better start than a third-round tie at home to Fourth Division Huddersfield Town! Sadly this becomes a typical FA Cup banana skin, as Fulham bow out of the competition at the first hurdle, losing 2–3 to a final Huddersfield goal in the last fifteen minutes. Our picture shows the close range shot from Viv Busby that secured our second equaliser. We can assure you Viv is in there amongst the bodies...somewhere.

Below: A posse of Nottingham Forest defenders and goalkeeper Peter Grummitt combine to keep the ball the right side of the goal-line. The ball is in there...somewhere. The Fulham attackers are recent signing Jackie Henderson (8) and John Doherty in his final game for Fulham. Henderson scored in the game, earning Fulham a 1–1 draw in March 1962. It was their first point following eleven consecutive defeats, a record losing run. However, the match proved to be a watershed and Fulham found enough form in the remaining matches to retain First Division status.

Here's the Queens Park Rangers side from 1966. Back row: Sibley, Hunt, Keetch, Springett, Kelly, Leach, Hazell and Langley; front row: Morgan, Allen, Morgan, Keen, Marsh and Wilks. But why a QPR squad in a Fulham book? Well, wily Alec Stock (later to become our manager) was then in charge of Rangers; he knew talent – and how to pluck it from Fulham. He had already secured Jim Langley on a free transfer and had picked up Rodney Marsh for a pittance. Finally he persuaded Bobby Keetch to join as well. All this was down to Fulham's new manager Vic Buckingham rapidly changing the personnel at the Cottage.

Further Fulham connections are Frank Sibley who assisted Kevin Keegan at Fulham and finally goalkeeping coach Mike Kelly. For the record this Rangers side took the Third Division by storm in 1967, and a season later they had made it straight into the First Division.

With today's officials equipped with microphones, we often see them covering up their lips to avoid television picking up what they're saying. Well, we just want to say that we invented the idea at Fulham forty years ago.

Left: A rare picture of Johnny Haynes and George Cohen together in 1967, and both players have signed the picture. Thanks to Brian Broughton for the photo.

In March 1981, new manager Malcolm Macdonald is starting to blood the young members of the squad, including goalkeeper Jim Stannard and Clive Day. This is the first appearance for Fulham of Dale Tempest, coming on as a substitute at Turf Moor. He's through on goal and looks certain to score a debut goal but is foiled by the diving Alan Stevenson and captain Brian Laws. The result at Burnley was the usual defeat.

 Below: But there is some success in this picture. On the right Robert Wilson wheels away after scoring against Wimbledon in February 1982, whilst Gordon Davies applauds the goal and the referee on the spot has no doubts about its validity. It was one of only five that 'Willo' scored in the league that season. Two Dean Coney goals and an own goal completed a miserable night for the Dons as Fulham won 4–1. On his knees and reflecting on 'one that got away' is future Fulham goalkeeping coach Dave Beasant.

A group of youth players photographed in about 1972. Quite a few progressed into the first team, though not as many as our memories would have us believe. Numbering everyone in the picture from left to right, these are the players who made it. Back row: 2 - Brian Greenaway; 4 - Tyrone James; 5 - Ernie Howe; front row: 3 - Steve Scrivens; 5 - John Fraser; 7 - Paul Shrubb; 9 - Terry Bullivant.

Below: all smiles as the club offers Christmas cheers in 1972. At back: John Cutbush, Fred Callaghan, Jimmy Dunne, Les Barrett, Steve Earle; front: Bill Taylor (coach), Barry Lloyd, Alan Mullery, Peter Mellor, John Mitchell, Paul Went, Ron Woolnough (physio) and Jimmy Conway.

Secretary George Noyce surveying his domain in the 1970s.

Below: It's a prelude to the 1978–79 season and Fulham are involved, as was usual in those days, in the Anglo-Scottish Cup. This is the final group match against Bristol City and a decent holiday crowd of nearly 4,500 has turned up to watch. Here an out-numbered Gordon Davies is denied an attempt at goal by a bicycle-kick clearance. He, like the team, had no luck on the day and City won 3–0. By losing two of the three group matches, Fulham didn't progress into the final stages that year. In fact, after the year they made the final (1975), they only once more progressed to the final stages.

Here's artwork from Fulham's Golden Years, Ashwater's first Fulham book produced in 1992. The book had a section which featured the 40 players who had made the most appearances for the club at the time. The group of players featured here are all the other players who had made at least 20 appearances.

A full list of their names is on the last page of this scrapbook.

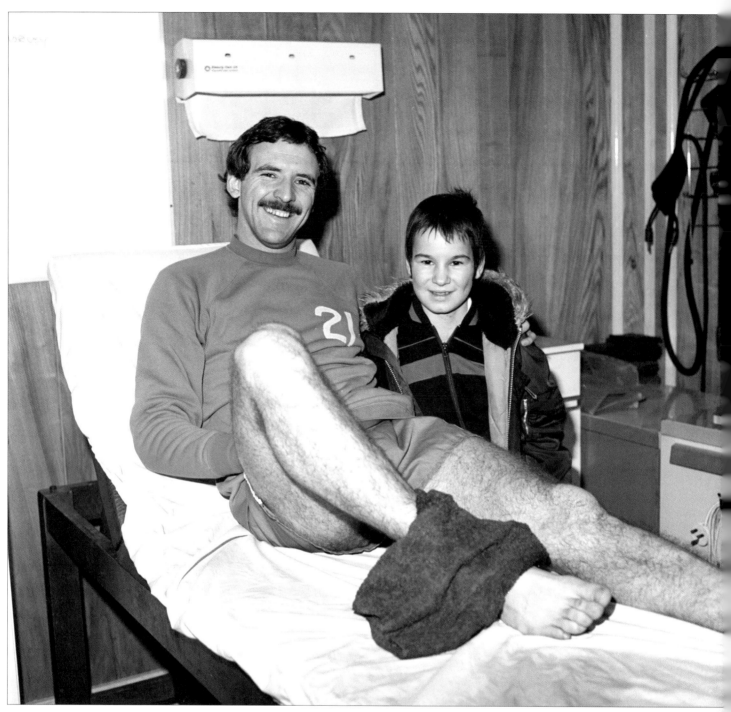

Players with fans.

Above: Gordon Davies on the treatment table is perked up by a visit from a young admirer (maybe his entire fan club...).

Right: That's Steve Earle (right) on a rare Christmas trip to England and back in his home territory of 'The Winning Post' pub in Whitton. Here he reminisces over old scrapbooks and ten years worth of exploits describing the 'happiest years of my life'.

Manager Malcolm Macdonald celebrates a deserved 'Manager of the Month' award, which involves a large bottle of whisky and posing for Ken's camera.

Below: Between 1980 and 1983, Fulham's rugby league club played on the hallowed Cottage turf. So here is a picture of the rugby boys, in their smart strip, playing at Wigan in April 1982, with John Wood leading a Fulham charge.

It's hard to be sure whose penalty area this is, such is the mix of forwards and defenders! One thing's for certain: it's a cold, rainy night at Ipswich in November 1973 – but over 20,000 have turned up to watch the League Cup replay. Second Division Fulham had outplayed Bobby Robson's First Division high-flyers in the first match at the Cottage but could only achieve a 2–2 draw. They were unfortunate in the replay too, being unluckily edged out 1–2; Steve Earle's final goal for Fulham wasn't quite enough. Here Paul Went leaps for a ball with Mick Lambert; also in the picture are Ipswich forward Trevor Whymark and defender Allan Hunter, with Fulham's Les Barrett looking poised for any 'second ball'.

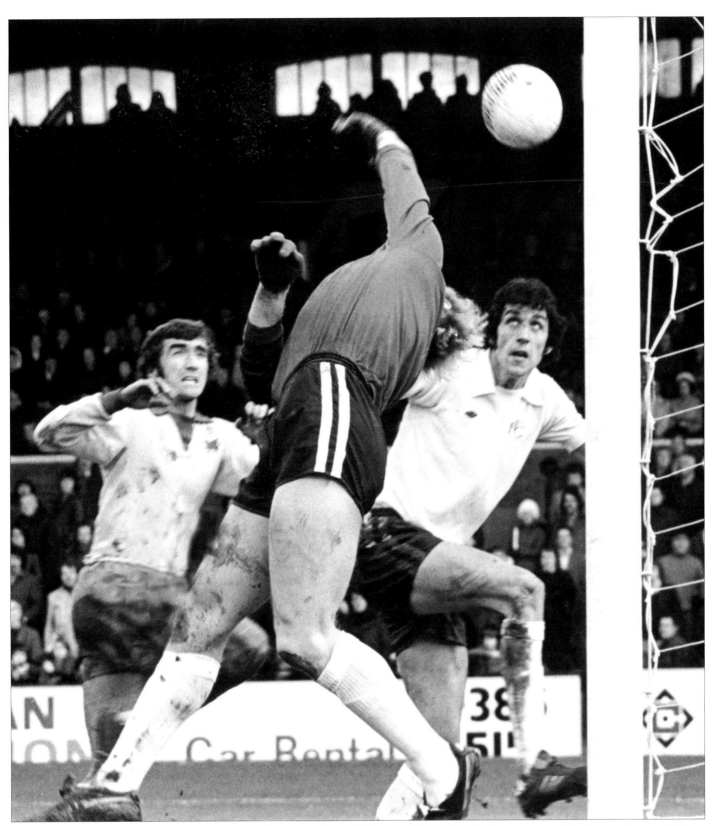

A Boxing Day morning encounter in 1974 with our London neighbours Orient. As often happens over Christmas, it wasn't the greatest of games and ended up as a goalless draw. It wasn't that festive either with six bookings! The 'nils' were down to two decent defences. Here Fulham goalkeeper Peter Mellor, playing well at the time, produces a reflex save to foil a rare Orient attack, with centre half John Lacy on hand to complete the clearance. Orient's Gerry Queen is lurking and hoping for a slip-up.

A pre-season photoshoot in 1969, with Les Barrett, Dave Roberts, Barry Lloyd and Dave Moreline performing for the photographers. On the ground at right is John Tyson, the real original of Fulham snappers.

Below: a glamorous interlude for our intrepid heroes as they play ball with a bevy of lovelies in 1966.

Right: One fan can't take it any more and walks out, preferring rain to the match.

It's December 1978 against Newcastle in change strip. It's a 1–3 defeat, but here's our goal. John Beck and John Evanson combine and an inch perfect cross arrives for Chris Guthrie (sans tooth) to throw himself at it to head a superb goal. The Magpies don't seem happy with the validity of the goal, but it counts. It was a goal against his first club and Guthrie was in a purple patch spell that would yield nine goals in ten league games, but unfortunately he and the team faded.

£25   FULHAM 2000   £25

TWENTY FIVE POUNDS

This is to certify that Mick Roots

helped to save Craven Cottage, the home of Fulham Football Club, by contributing to FULHAM 2000 the above sum, and is entitled to any benefits which may accrue commensurate with this contribution.

GEOFFREY FAULKNER
TREASURER, FULHAM 2000

JOHNNY HAYNES
PATRON

TONY GALE
Central Defender, 1977-84
318 appearances; 21 goals

Membership No. 3295

00041

A couple of Micks. Above: Mick Petrovic was delighted to receive a signed note from manager Alec Stock.

Left: Mick Roots reminds us of the efforts of Fulham 2000 to save the club; the supporter based organisation issued certificates acknowledging contributions.

Johnny Byrne swivels and scores against Huddersfield Town in Johnny Haynes' first match in charge as player-manager in November 1968. It was a topsy-turvy game in which Fulham went behind, were level three times and finally went ahead to run out 4–3 victors. It was Byrne's first goal for the club and in that same match Vic Halom and Cliff Jones also scored their first goals for Fulham.

Below: An exhausted Haynes shakes the hand of his England colleague Byrne at the end of the game and the end of a traumatic week that had seen the sacking of Bobby Robson. Even after victory, the weight of responsibility seems to rest heavily on Haynes' shoulders. It came as no surprise that his managerial reign lasted just four games, as his new post was something he never really sought.

Johnny wakes up Fulham

By Sam Bartram

FULHAM 4, HUDDERSF'LD 3

JOHNNY HAYNES says he has taken the job of managing Fulham "reluctantly" . . . but in this win he tackled their troubles with a real thirst for a fight.

Haynes was magnificent, shouting and urging, direct-

This is 1980 and the start of Fulham's rise under Malcolm Macdonald. This is his squad. Back row: Roger Thompson (coach), Clive Day, Kevin Lock, Gary Peters, Steve Hatter, Tony Gale, Doug Hatcher, Perry Digweed, Roger Brown, Geoff Banton, Tony Mahoney, Ron Woolnough (physio); front row: Malcolm Macdonald (manager), John Beck, Sean O'Driscoll, Gordon Davies, Les Strong, Brian Corner, Brian Gibson, Tommy Mason, Robert Wilson.

Below: Clive Walker puts away a penalty against Huddersfield in February 1989, sending the goalkeeper the wrong way. Just over 4,000 had turned up to watch the match; they must have known something, as Fulham lost 1–2. Maybe it was the sandy beach of a goalmouth that inhibited our heroes.

Richard Money gets in on the act with a rare goal picture for him. This diving header puts the seal on a 2–0 win in an early kick off match against Sheffield United on a sunny Good Friday in March 1978. The first score was an own goal credited officially to Colin Franks, but some journalists had the 'oggy' as down to ex-Fulham defender John Cutbush.

Below: a TV snap of Bobby Zamora's mis-hit shot to secure a historic injury-time winner against Arsenal in January 2012. The Gunners had dominated early on and had gone ahead. Fulham came much more into the game, but were still behind with twelve minutes to go. However, Steve Sidwell (a former Arsenal youth player) levelled with a header, allowing Zamora to crown an excellent Whites performance. It was a real Premiership highlight night that few will forget.

Gordon Davies – always a threat on opposition goals.

The great Alec Stock was our manager around our Cup Final year of 1975, but he had previously visited the Cottage in 1958 when he was manager of non-League Yeovil Town (as the programme pointed out). Note the pre-floodlights kick-off time for the match of 2.15, ensuring a finish at around 4pm, when you could just about see!

For the record, this turned out to be a routine 4–0 win for the Whites, on the way to the FA Cup semi-final (unlike our later cup tie with Yeovil in 1993, enough said).

Alec had been player/manager of Yeovil Town in 1949 when, in the fourth round of the FA Cup, they produced one of the great shocks by beating Len Shackleton's First Division giants Sunderland 2–1 on the sloping Huish pitch. Alec scored the first goal.

Below: Alec always had time for the fans.

Villa and Southampton fame, came in. Billy brought greater distinction than ever to Yeovil, and it was a blow to the club when he left them.

Then, however, Yeovil created more history. They appointed the youngest player-manager of a professional club in the country, 27-years-old Alec Stock. Before he left Alec had equalled the record of his predecessors Page, Halliday and Kingdon by taking Yeovil to the Third round of the F.A. Cup for the fourth time.

Kit Symons watches – and then celebrates – Chris Coleman's goal in the 3–0 victory over Gillingham in April 1999. It followed a mis-kicked back-heel that the defender and the goalkeeper left for each other, and the ball just trickled in.

But here's Kit in less than celebratory mood as he is sent off at Burnley in May 1999.

Mark Maunders has been a stalwart of the Fulham staff for many years, liaising with players and doing good work behind the scenes. His taste in choosing a baseball cap may be questioned, but at least he has the decency to wear it the right way round.

Below: Manager Kevin Keegan was always prepared to sign autographs, as here at York City's ground. (No, that's not Shane Warne in the yellow jacket...)

Opposite: *Simon Morgan, goalkeeper Tony Lange and Mark Blake combine to clear a Carlisle attack in August 1996. Fulham win 1–0 and eventually complete the double over the Cumbrian side. Both sides were promoted at the end of the season; Fulham went on to better things, but the Carlisle club was relegated at the end of the following season.*

Davies
delight

By SAM BARTRAM

Fulham 3 Leicester 0

Davies got his first
before half-time al-
though he looked off-
side when chasing a
long clearance from
Lock. And his second

A packed Craven Cottage under the floodlights.

Left: action from the match against Leicester City in April 1979. Watched by Peter Kitchen, our Welsh terrier Gordon Davies gets in a shot from the edge of the penalty area. Our intrepid photographer cannot remember whether this was one of Gordon's two goals that day in the 3–0 win, but we'll claim it! Sneaking in the picture is famous referee Clive Thomas.

Right: only £1 (including VAT) to watch Fulham's famous FA Cup semi-final match at Hillsborough in 1975, but the ticket, which belongs to Kevin O'Callaghan, is now almost priceless as it has been signed by Fulham's goalscorer on the day, John Mitchell.

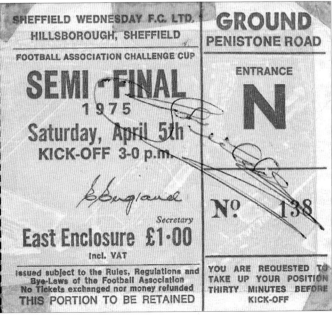

Here are grounds that Fulham have visited in the last 20 years. So the simple question is, can you name them all? The answers are on the last page of the book.

A Pipex team with printed players' signatures – though not many are recognisable without the namecheck!

Les Strong sneaks into the scrapbook once again, this time flying high in defence. Below right: Two hands and one foot are together not enough to thwart Barry Hayles.

Mike Smith with ticket office girls, Sandra and Gill.

It all began here. Tony Gale signs professional forms in June 1976, watched by club secretary Graham Hortop.

This is Fulham.

Jimmy Conway gets away from QPR's Tony Hazell and Don Givens in the last match of the 1972–73 season. Fulham ended the season in mid-table, but QPR finished as runners-up and were promoted to the top flight.

After beating Macclesfield in the FA Cup in Bobby Robson's first game in charge, our reward was a home tie against Second Division Portsmouth in February 1968. On a cold, windy day a massive 40,000 crowd turned up to watch in expectation. Portsmouth's fans occupied the whole of the Cottage end and the Pompey chimes rang out. However, it turned out to be an awful game on a bumpy pitch in which defences utterly dominated, with both sides determined not to lose. Here, key striker Allan Clarke flashes in a shot, but like most it went wide. The result was an inevitable goalless draw. Action from the replay is shown on page 16.

Below: Newcastle full back John Craggs' head drops and goalkeeper Gordon Marshall is helpless on the ground. Clarke has just taken advantage of a defensive mix-up in the Geordies' box to score the first goal early in the match in February 1967. The ball has already been lashed into the net and bounced out again. Clarke (in an away kit at home) is sporting his usual goal salute; he was in spectacular form on the day, scoring a hat trick and unlucky not to get more. A frail Newcastle side were fortunate to leave the Cottage that day with just a 5–1 defeat.

Geoff Horsfield cements Fulham's victory over Gillingham in April 1999 with a shot following up his saved penalty. The 3–0 win over the Kent team took Fulham to the point where promotion was in sight.

Below: action from Johnny Haynes in the match against Sheffield Wednesday in January 1962. On the right in the left-hand picture is centre half and England colleague Peter Swan (number 5 in the other photo). In that same year, Swan along with team-mates Tony Kay and David 'Bronco' Layne were involved in a betting scandal that rocked football at the time. They bet on their own team to lose against lowly Ipswich Town, which they did 0–2. Swan was 27 and at the height of his career but received a four-month jail sentence in 1964 and a life ban from football. That ban was commuted to eight years in 1972, and Swan, then almost 36, returned to play for Sheffield Wednesday in the opening match of the 1972–73 season – against Fulham, of course. He made fifteen appearances that season for Wednesday; however the team's form faded and Swan lost his place in the side, and he didn't play again for the Owls.

Paul Trollope scores one of Fulham's four goals in the win at Kenilworth Road in March 1999. This goal at Luton was followed by another in the next match three days later, against Bristol Rovers in the pouring night rain, which put him on a hot scoring streak! Paul netted only five goals for Fulham and all but one were away from Craven Cottage.

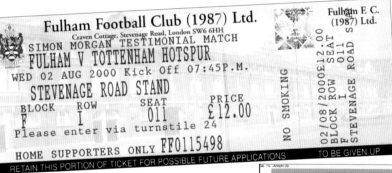

FULHAM FOOTBALL CLUB (1987) LIMITED

BARCLAYS LEAGUE DIVISION 2

FULHAM V BRADFORD CITY

13 MAR 1993   K.O. 03:00

MILLER STAND
BLOCK   ROW   SEAT COMPLIMENTARY
W   I   031

TO BE RETAINED

FULHAM FOOTBALL CLUB
SEASON 1980/81

Season Ticket

MATCH No. **13**

13   BLOCK

This voucher must be torn
from this book in the
presence of the gateman.   J

FULHAM FOOTBALL CLUB

THE BOARDROOM

07/04/2003

FULHAM F.C.
DEVELOPMENT ASSOCIATION

G   3512

Name ....

Address ....

Counterfoils to be
returned by Wednesday,
March 20th, 1974

FULHAM F.C.
DEVELOPMENT ASSOCIATION
Promoter - W. GOODSELL
Craven Cottage, Stevenage Road, Fulham, S.W. 6.   G   3512

Grand National Draw
(Race run at Liverpool on Sat., 30th March, 1974 (or when run))
FIRST HORSE
ONE HUNDRED POUNDS
SECOND HORSE   THIRD HORSE   FOURTH HORSE
£50   £25   £10
ALL OTHER RUNNERS AT THE OFF £2.00 EACH

Draw for Horses held at CRAVEN COTTAGE, FULHAM, S.W. 6.
ON THURSDAY, MARCH 21st, 1974
3p   Promoted in accordance with Small Lotteries and Gaming Act 1956.
All proceeds to go to the benefit of the Club. This ticket is receipt for donation.

A rare picture of forward Mike Brown, who played just four games for Fulham, 1961–63 Here he vies for possession with a West Bromwich defender.

Did the ball hit the post? Did it go in the goal? Well, neither actually. Les Barrett, nearest to the goal-line, fires in a shot that passes inches wide of the post. This was a 1–3 defeat at Carlisle in April 1972, which kept us firmly in the danger zone. On the day Earle and Conway were unavailable, which left us with Stan Horne and Fred Callaghan up front. However, two scruffy goalless draws in the final two matches meant the Whites avoided relegation by the skin of their teeth.

Gordon Davies celebrates one of his two goals in the 4–1 home defeat of Exeter in October 1981. The attendance was a mere 4,500.

Another picture from the Exeter match featured opposite. We can assure our readers that in amongst the Exeter players is our own Roger Brown, scoring our fourth goal.

Below: a rare appearance for Richard Money in the scrapbook, seen here in action against Wrexham in October 1979. Terry Bullivant, also rarely seen, is at the back of the picture. Former Arsenal centre half John Roberts is in the picture (next to Bullivant) as well as striker Mick Vinter (foreground) who always seemed to play well against us, especially when with Notts County. It wasn't our greatest day, and we lost at home to the Welsh club for the second successive season, this time 0–2.

A young Brian 'Pat' O'Connell tries to get the ball under control in the Cardiff penalty area in November 1961; Maurice Cook and Haynes wait for developments. In the background it's a rare glimpse of Trevor 'Tosh' Chamberlain. It was a grim day; the Whites lost 0–1 to the Bluebirds, who were eventually relegated.

We seem to recall that soon after this, the price of the Flutter tickets doubled to £2. Hardly anyone thought it a good idea, and the Flutter just fluttered away.

The week after George Best arrived at the club Fulham entertained Wolves, but hopes of a hatful of goals were dashed and we played out a goalless draw. This was in September 1976. Here Ernie Howe watches Wolves' Steve Kindon failing to connect with a swirling cross. Wolves ended the season as champions.

Two views of the ground. Above: Excavations begin at the Putney end prior to the construction of the Riverside Stand in 1971. Below: the ground sparkling in the sunshine a few years later, with the Riverside Stand built.

A couple of Matthewsons. Above: Reg scores against Torquay on a Friday night in February 1971. It was his only goal for the club, and he contrived to hide himself behind a post in the picture. Below: Watched by referee Gordon Hill and the late great Eusebio, Reg gets in a fine tackle on a Benfica forward on the opening night of the Riverside Stand in 1972.

Joy follows our goal against Lincoln in May 1982, which secured our promotion to Division Two.

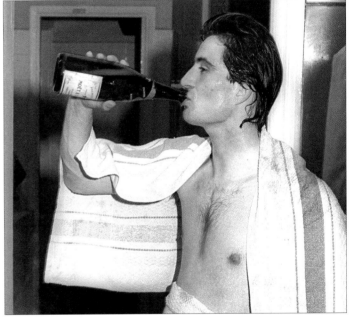

From Jimmy Conway's corner, John Dempsey manages to squeeze his header away from goalkeeper John Milkins (on the six-yard line) and despite two defenders on the goal-line and five others around, the ball still goes in. Debutant Vic Halom watches the action. By a misty Thames, Fulham earn a point in a 2–2 draw with Portsmouth in November 1968, but they should have won.

It was John Dempsey's last goal for Fulham. Fulham's other scorer that day was Fred Callaghan, and his goal is commemorated in the 'hug' picture on page 11.

Dempsey's final game for Fulham, in the following January, was the reverse fixture at Fratton Park.

Allan Clarke has just scored against Tottenham in October 1966 with a shot from the edge of the box and his effort is greeted by a stream of toilet rolls, almost obligatory at the time. The linesman dashes back to the halfway line. Umbrellas are everywhere and even one of the photographers feels the need for protection from the rain.

    Below: Perhaps for throwing the toilet rolls or maybe for enthusiastically running on to the pitch, two young lads are led around the touchline and escorted from the ground by the long arm of the law. (Dear reader: do you recognise yourself. If so, do get in touch!)

    The damp day is obvious looking at the apparel and faces of those in the Hammersmith End; the soggy theme continued to the end of the match, as Fulham lost by three goals to four.

Above: A mess-up in the Hull defence at Boothferry Park in April 1981 produces the only goal of the match. The scorer is Roger Brown (in dark shirt) on the ground; leaping away is Kevin Lock.

Left: For those viewing in black and white, Fulham are next to the Brentford team playing uniquely in green at the Cottage in February 1981.

Below: After two postponements and wasted trips, Fulham go to Bramall Lane for a fourth round FA Cup replay in March 1967. Fulham were unlucky in the home tie, but soon find themselves two down in the replay against Sheffield United. However Fred Callaghan brings Fulham back in it early in the second half with a twenty-five yard shot that goalkeeper Alan Hodgkinson never sees and which thuds in off a post. Goalscorer Callaghan is at far left in the picture. The linesman is flagging furiously for offside against Johnny Haynes or Steve Earle, but he is over-ruled, presumably because the Fulham players were 'not interfering'. Fulham push for an equaliser but finally succumb 1–3 to a second goal from a veteran, former Norwich City reserve Bill Punton.

Tony Gale in typically resolute pose tries to get another Fulham move going during the match at Gillingham in April 1982. Despite a successful season, the Priestfield Stadium was never the luckiest or easiest places to visit in more ways than one. This was no exception and it proved a blip in the promotion season with Gillingham winning by the only goal.

Two stalwarts from the 1980s. Peter Scott (above) played over 300 matches for the club. Cliff Carr, here pictured in England colours (he won an England U21 cap in 1985), played over 150 games.

A Ray Lew page.

Above: With his usual aplomb, Ray converts a penalty as part of a 3–1 win over Newport County in October 1981. Gordon Davies, almost inevitably, scored the other two against his native Welsh opposition.

Below: Heading for promotion, Fulham are expected to beat lowly Reading two months later. On a very windy day that destroys decent football, Fulham find themselves behind against a defensively-minded Royals side. However, in the dying embers of the game, Ray Lewington pops up from nowhere to salvage a point in a 2–2 draw – hurrah!

Sometimes things don't go to plan... Here on this page are two goals against us in April 1966. The good news is that we eventually won both matches. Above is a goal from West Bromwich's Jeff Astle. Below is a goal from David Ford of Sheffield Wednesday; goalkeeper Jack McClelland is well beaten.

In both pictures Brian Nichols is stranded and forlorn on the goal-line; and at right in both pictures Stan Brown is equally crestfallen.

Oh, no, a Burnley goal against us in September 1961. Seven dejected Fulham players – Dodgin, Mullery, Lowe, Haynes, Cook, O'Connell and Cohen – watch as the visitors celebrate yet another goal in their 5–3 victory at the Cottage. Burnley finished as runners-up to the champions, scoring over 100 goals in the process.

Oh, no, a Burnley goal against us in March 1982. Gerry Peyton is grounded and Robert Wilson, Roger Brown and Les Strong are helpless. Burnley captain Brian Flynn looks a little more pleased. Fulham managed to save the day with the inevitable Gordon Davies goal, and it was another point closer to Division Two.

Two views of Dean Court from October 1969, when both Fulham and Bournemouth were in the Third Division.

Above: Top-scorer Jimmy Conway cuts into the penalty area, leaving a defender trailing. The referee watching was one of the best around at the time, Mr DW Smith from Stonehouse in Gloucestershire.

Below: Fred Callaghan, up with the forwards, fires in a left-foot shot watched by Johnny Haynes. In the background can be seen the old-fashioned alphabetical scoreboard, the Sixties way of giving the half-time scores.

For the record, an entertaining 2–2 draw ensued on the south coast, with both Fulham's leading scorers, Earle and Conway, finding the net. Playing for Bournemouth was the ace goalscorer Ted MacDougall – who also inevitably scored.

Defender Geoff Banton clears from Sheffield United's experienced Bob Hatton on Boxing Day 1980.

Below: In 1998 Manager Kevin Keegan persuaded the thirty-seven year old former England international Peter Beardsley to be part of his team building at Craven Cottage. The picture is from a League Cup tie in August 1998 at Ninian Park Cardiff, where he signs autographs for happy fans. Beardsley had scored in the first leg when Fulham had won 2–1 at Craven Cottage. Fulham also won this second leg 2–1, to go through to meet Premiership Southampton, whom they also beat. Beardsley played just eleven times for Fulham that season before joining Hartlepool United to end his career after twenty years.

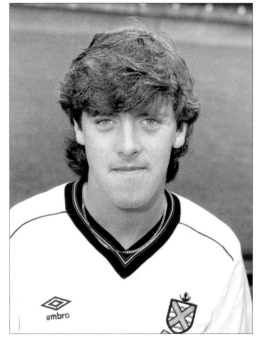

Steve Finnan. Brian Cottington. and photographer Ken Simpson, often confused with Ken Coton. Below: when the Supporters' Club had a football team – and what a record when Fulham fan Peter Woodman was in the team! Below right: Alec Stock is pictured with Sir Stanley Rous, president of FIFA.

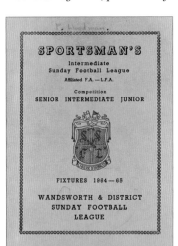

Les Barrett and Stan Brown hone their skills during training in 1968, when Fulham used the Harrods Sports Ground, now the Harrodian School.

Photos by: NICK TOMEY.

SEAN FARRELL was unlucky with this effort against Mansfield.

LEE TIERLING makes the early running last Saturday.

Supported by
BONUSPRINT®

'Victory at last'. Our jubilant players salute the terrific away following at the end of last Saturday's game.

Supported by
BONUSPRINT®

Martin Pike shot well over from Hails' cross, and Mark Kelly was caught reluctantly right footed after a promising Pike run. Half time came and went, and fortunately Fulham came back with a bit of vigour.

Hails swivelled his way past two defenders, but the move disintegrated after that. Jeff Eckhardt headed a Newson cross down for Brazil, whose shot came back hard off the 'keeper.

Half an hour before the end Stannard saved well from Stephen Torpey. The Fulham 'keeper hadn't had much to do before that. For most of the second half most of the action was at the Bradford end and it wasn't long before Eckhardt nodded on for Hails who charged his sixth of the season into the back of Tomlinson's goal.

He almost made it seven a few minutes later. A flashy Farrell flick-on found Kelly whose cross was cleared. Hails picked it up but his shot was straight at the Bradford 'keeper.

Player/Manager Frank Stapleton came on to see if he could be the difference between the two teams. In fact, only goal difference separated these sides before the game, and the situation hadn't changed at the end.

Fulham: *Stannard, Morgan, Pike, Nebbeling, Newson, Thomas, Hails, Marshall, Farrell, Brazil, Kelly (Ferney). Subs not used: Tucker.*

Bradford: *Tomlinson, Williams, Haseltine, Duxbury, Oliver, Hoyle, Jewell, Duxbury W., McCarthy, Torpey, Reid. Subs: Tinnion, Stapleton.*

EMMA HAWKEY

High flying Stoke must have been unpleasantly surprised by their visitor's game. When they weren't being astonished by our goalkeeper, everyone in the press box was asking after Fulham's number eleven. Mark Kelly took care of Stoke's tricky winger Russell, **and** orchestrated the general movement forward. Mark Tucker coped well with his unexpected First Team run. Our line-up may have been makeshift, but it didn't look it.

But still no goals. Hails brought the ball forward for Farrell, whose lofted shot was headed over by John Marshall. That was a nice, gentle, Fulhamish move.

A hard, low Marshall cross was too hard and low for Sean Farrell, running into the Stoke area. Our best chance came just after Stoke took the lead. Sean Farrell sent what looked like a mixture between a cross and a shot, curling in towards Grobbelaar's goal, but the Zimbabwean international tipped it over the bar.

Just before the end Udo Onwere redirected a Kelly free kick straight into the Stoke 'keeper's arms. And so it was that Fulham headed back to London point-less and defeated, but knowing that if they could play like that against Brighton on Tuesday they would surely win.

Stoke: *Grobbelaar, Butler, Hockaday, Cranson, Sandford, Gleghorn, Foley, Russell, Stein, Shaw, Beeston. Subs: Ware, Regis.*

Fulham: *Stannard, Tucker, Pike, Onwere, Newson, Thomas, Hails, Marshall, Farrell, Brazil, Kelly. Subs: Ferney, Cooper.*

EMMA HAWKEY

WIMBLEDON 0 FULHAM 0
Neville Ovenden Football Combination
Monday, 19th April, 1993

Fulham reserves played a weaker than usual Wimbledon side and managed to hold them to a goalless draw. With ex-Cottager Perry Digweed in the Doris goal, and two Wimbledon trialists (Swift and Mosley) playing for Fulham, that ironic back drop provided just about the only interest in a game almost without incident.

Peter Baah's first minute effort went straight to the Wimbledon 'keeper, and that was a taste of the blandness to come. A truly excellent tackle by Mark Tucker stopped Leyton Allen 8 or 9 yards out and prevented an almost certain goal.

Alan Gough remained untroubled for most of the game, and so did Digweed. Kelly Haag failed to read a good ball in from Peter Baah, and then player-manager Sparrow shot well wide of the Fulham goal.

After the interval Bedrossian and Onwere replaced Baah and Jupp, but the game continued in the same vein. Fulham's best chance came from a free kick from 35 yards. Bedrossian's shot forced a save from Digweed in the sixtieth minute.

Wimbledon: *Digweed, Brooker, Fleming, Castledine, Perry, Skinner, Fiori, Fell, Allen, Anthrobus, Sparrow. Subs: Finegan, Cunningham.*

Fulham: *Gough, Jupp, Lewis L., Armytage, Tucker, Mosley, Lewis J. Ferney, Haag, Swift, Baah. Subs: Bedrossian, Onwere.*

Referee: *John Moore, Norwich.*

two seasons later and the two sides met in the F.A. Cup Semi Finals. The first match at Villa Park drew a crowd of 59,989. Graham Leggatt put Fulham in front only for John Connelly to equalise for the Clarets. Fulham were by all accounts the better side that day but in the replay at Filbert Street Burnley came out on top 2-1.

Turf Moor is one of our bogey grounds. We have lost in fifteen of our last eighteen visits. The game earlier this season proved no better despite two goals from Sean Farrell we lost 5-2. At Craven Cottage it has been a different story despite the odd Burnley success. In October 1977 Tony Mahoney scored his first for the club in a 4-1 home win though he will wish to forget the encounter exactly three years later when he was sent off as we went down 2-0.

It was our second successive dismissal against the Clarets, a year earlier Peter Marinello had been shown the red card by Referee Ron Challis but this only served to inspire a 3-1 win. Gordon Davies (2) and Kevin Lock the men on target. Burnley also lost 3-1 last time they came to Craven Cottage with current assistant boss Ray Lewington twice on target before Ray Houghton scored a cracking goal to seal the points.

Chelsea will probably win the Combination championship while Fulham seemed destined for the wooden spoon. Nobody would have thought this during the first half but nobody would have doubted it during the second.

170 spectators were present at this match, certainly the second highest home reserve gate of the season. Few of these would, I feel, like to assess this Jekyll and Hyde performance. All would agree, however, that in Ara Bedrossian, Fulham had the most naturally skilful player on the field.

Fulham: Gough, Jupp, L. Lewis, P. Kelly, Nebbeling, Tucker, Ferney, Bedrossian, Haworth, Richards, Baah. Used substitutes: J. Lewis and Hawkins.

Chelsea: Carroll, Skiverton, Myers, Pearce, Duberry, Lee, Hopkin, Burley, Shipperley, Fleck, Norman. Unused substitutes: Rowe, Izzet.

Referee: Mr. B. L. Polkey.

Port Vale: *Musselwhite, Sandeman, Sulley, Walker, Swan, Glover, Kerr (Van Der Laan), Aspin, Cross (Kent), Foyle, Taylor.*

Fulham: *Harrison, Newson, Pike, Eckhardt, Ferney (Tierling), Thomas, Cooper, Marshall, Hails, Baah (Kelly P.), Onwere.*

Referee: *Mr. S. D. Bell.*

JULIAN HAILS *beats former Fulham favourite Clive Walker to the ball at the Goldstone Ground.*

GAVIN NEBBELING *made sure we won this ball at the Goldstone Ground.*

tos by: NICK TOMEY.

Skipper **SIMON MORGAN** *clears his lines in acrobatic fashion on the way to victory at Exeter.*

Chest against Chester nice one Gary! **PIC BY NICK TOMEY**

BERT HAWORTH scoring our only goal against Tottenham Hotspur.

DOMINIC GUARD

Swansea: *Freestone, Lyttle, Jenkins, Walker, Harris, Coughlin, Hayes (Bowen 58), Wimbleton, West, Cornforth (Ford 80), Legg.*
Fulham: *Stannard, Morgan, Pike, Eckhardt, Newson, Thomas, Hails, Marshall, Cooper, McGlashan (Ferney 45), Onwere. Sub not used: Tierling.*
Booked: *Harris.*
Referee: *R. Hamer (Bristol).*

JULIAN HAILS *who scored our deserved equaliser.*

UDO ONWERE *was quickly into action after coming on as substitute against Stoke City.* **PIC BY NICK TOMEY**

GARY BRAZIL

"That'll bring the crowds back!" quipped John Yems, who was pleased to get this first win under his belt, especially with such a young team. Ben Hawkins, Nicky Andrews and Danny Bolt all did well, while of the older lads Gary Murphy had another good game and Alan Hendricks gave more tantalising glimpses of what might yet be with the right attitude.

"A few heartstoppers and we gave away a couple of silly goals", was John's summing-up, "but considering the weakened side we had, I thought the boys did really well. They tried hard, worked for one another and the spirit is getting them through at the moment. Once again, a credit to the way they've been coached".

FULHAM (4-4-2): *James Power, Hawkins, Jupp, Murphy, Carey, Bolt, Mison, Ray Power, Andrews, Richards and Haworth. Sub: Hendricks (for Haworth, 22 mins).*

IAN CRANNA

Messrs. **STANNARD, PIKE** *and* **TUCKER** *guarding Mark Stein.*

Mullery, England and Knowles all hold their breath as a Fulham shot from Steve Earle beats Pat Jennings but whistles past an upright. It's October 1966 and another classic encounter with north London rivals Spurs. As in the previous game in February, the match produces another seven-goal thriller with Spurs once again edging it 3–4 in a topsy-turvy encounter where the lead changed hands often. It featured on The Big Match and Peter Lorenzo waxed lyrical about the game and in particular Fulham's young striker Allan Clarke.

Below: In front of a sparsely populated Villa Park terrace in March 1966 Graham Leggat ghosts past three Aston Villa defenders watched by Johnny Haynes. The Scottish international was in fine form, scoring in just the second minute and then adding another later in the game as Fulham ran riot 5–2.

Philippe Albert leaps highest to score with a powerful header against Wigan as Fulham win 2–0 against the Latics in April 1999. Albert was almost thirty-two but still a classy performer. Injuries had limited his playing time at Newcastle and Fulham boss Kevin Keegan persuaded the north-east club to loan Albert until the end of the season to assist in the promotion drive. He played thirteen games and scored two goals, before returning to Belgium to play out the final season of his career. It's a good job central defenders were around that day as Kit Symons netted the other!

Below: a rare picture of Rufus Brevett in the same month giving it a hundred per cent as usual and firing in a left-wing cross after a run down the flank. This is at Chesterfield where on the day the promotion campaign stuttered a little and the Whites went down 0–1.

Here's the story behind this picture sent to us by Kevin O'Callaghan – an evocative picture of a grim time in Fulham's history, but can you spot the ball...? Kevin writes: 'This was the Bradford game on Boxing Day 1990 at the Cottage. It was a Division Three fixture, it was the Alan Dicks era, and Fulham were struggling. A crowd of 3,029 left their cold turkey to watch the game, which itself resembled cold turkey. I took my eldest son, Aidan. It was his first ever game and it was freezing. At that time the players didn't do fitness drills before the game. At five to three they came out and kicked a few balls about, and the forwards would ping in a few shots to warm up Big Jim Stannard. Aidan watched all this closely and when the ref blew for the toss of the coin he announced "Can we go home now?" I should have listened to him; the game was a poor 0–0 draw and we almost had hypothermia by the end.'

A selection of recent memorabilia collected by Gillian Ray.

Supporter Dave Wilson is rather proud to have kept this autographed football from the 1981–82 Division Three runners-up squad, from which we show a selection of famous names: Jim Stannard, Ray Houghton, Tony Gale, Cliff Carr and Roger Brown.

Below: This is Boxing Day 1980 and a rather un-festive picture. Fulham are just about to clinch victory with a 2–1 win over Sheffield United when an incident flares up in the visitors' goalmouth in the last minute. Gordon Davies is involved and Tony Mahoney (never far from trouble) is in the melee. When calm is restored referee Martin from Hampshire has no hesitation and sends off Sheffield United's Mike Trusson.

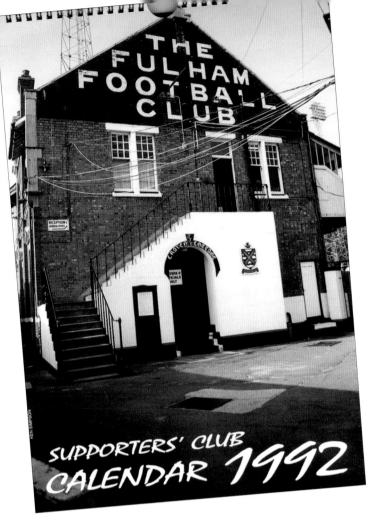

SUPPORTERS' CLUB CALENDAR 1992

Your Matchday Host: Les Strong

The effervescent Les Strong joined Fulham as a junior player in 1969 having been spotted by Youth Team Manager George Cohen.

Although he started his career as a pencil-thin right-winger, Les established himself as a solid defender.

After turning professional in 1971, he played in over 450 first team games putting him in Fulham's top ten all time appearances list. Les commanded the back line and played at his best alongside Bobby Moore in Fulham's run to Wembley 1975. Ironically, the final was one of just 13 games he missed in a nine year period.

Made Club Captain in 1980 by Malcolm McDonald, he left in 1983 to join Fred Callaghan at Brentford. He then finished his playing career in 1984 after a season with Alan Mullery at Crystal Palace.

Any enquiries?
By phone: 020 8336 7555   By email: hospitality@fulhamfc.com   or visit our website: www.fulham.com

Les Strong effervescent?
Confirmation that we are customers?
What happened to the printed Fultime – and to the new White?
Thanks to a special fan who helped on the Haynes book and promoted it in the Latymer Old Students magazine.
An ambivalent letter from David Mellor – a Fulham friend or foe?

fultime
ORANJE IS HET NIEUWE ZWART

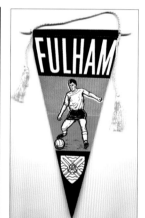

FULHAM PROMOTED to DIV. 2 1971

FULHAM customer charter 2003/04

Thank you very much for your letter about Fulham.

Sadly there is nothing I would like more than for Fulham to stay on at Craven Cottage. I fear the dice are inevitably loaded against them because there isn't the same pressure for the Club to stay as there was with Chelsea, and the Craven Cottage site, being on the river, is so much more attractive for re-development. But certainly, I shall not want to be anything other than constructive on this, and am ready to help out in any way that might be useful.

were placed on the graves of Ashworth and Dolbe in Edmonton Cemetery.

Johnny Haynes 'The Maestro'

Sheila Seymour, an old friend of Johnny Haynes, sent a letter to Latymer some time ago asking for assistance in researching the life of Johnny for his biography. Andrew Granath, School Archivist, started the ball rolling by trawling through Latymer's archives for references to him and put Sheila in touch with other Old Students who contributed. They are all named in the book's list of acknowledgements.

The book has now been published and on the 7th May 2008 Sheila came to London with her husband for the book launch that evening in Fulham. We were delighted that they took time during the day to visit the School and give two free copies to the School Library.

Sheila reported that the book launch in Fulham went well with over 100 attending, including Tom Wilson, who is Sir Bobby Robson's best friend.

Author Martin Plumb and Fulham photographer Ken Coton have combined to produce this tribute to the career of JOHNNY HAYNES. Anyone who would like to buy a copy, can find details at www.ashwaterpress.co.uk

Miranda McAllister, School Librarian, and Andrew Granath, being presented with two copies of 'The Maestro' from Sheila Seymour (centre) in the Ashworth Library May 2008

For his coverage of the match against Burnley in August 1978, photographer Ken Coton decided to load up with colour film and put a long lens on his camera. He managed to capture action pictures of Gordon Davies and Geoff Banton. It proved to be a good decision to train his camera on midfield, as Ken didn't miss any goals, the match ending up as a goalless draw. The picture of Gordon featured on the programme cover during the 1978–79 season.

Here are two pages of pictures featuring Fulham's great centre forward Bedford Jezzard, who later became manager in 1958. Our thanks to supporter Derek Hicks for these gems.

The action photograph is signed; below that picture the manager checks out an injured Graham Leggat.

The young lady below, with Bobby Robson, Jezzard and Johnny Haynes, is actress Janette Scott (daughter of Thora Hird).

Two team pictures featuring Jezzard. Above is the 1949–50 squad who played in Fulham's first ever season in the top flight.

These are the players. Back row: Ayres, Freeman, Quested, Flack, Kelly, Taylor, Bacuzzi, Penn (trainer); front: Stevens, Thomas, Rowley, Dodgin (manager) Jezzard, McDonald, Bewley.

The picture on the right is a fine picture showing a bunch of fine men, but we are not quite sure what it was in aid of. We thought they were all Fulham players, and we can recognise George Cohen (second left at back) and on his left, Maurice Cook. Jezzard is in the centre of the picture, with John Doherty to his right. Some other players look familiar, but they may not be connected with the club at all.

March 1978 and John Mitchell gets in front of his marker to flash in a header against Luton Town. Only 8,000 were there to see Fulham win 1–0 with a looping header from twelve yards by Tony Mahoney. On the night Mahoney (not in picture) wore unusually the number four shirt. On the far left is Luton's John Faulkner who had been signed by Leeds after a great display against them for Sutton United in the FA Cup. However, he couldn't dislodge Jack Charlton, but following his transfer to Luton played over 200 league games for the Hatters.

Opposite page: *a sight we always like to see – the ball in the opposition net.*

Below: a 4–0 rout of Burnley at Craven Cottage just before Christmas 1998. Simon Morgan scores twice before half time. The first is an impressive header, his second, shown here, is a little more fortunate. Steve Hayward's corner finds Chris Coleman; his effort isn't cleared and Morgs stabs home a close-range shot with a slight deflection that takes it the other side of the diving goalkeeper.

Toto sang the song 'Hold the line' – and Shrewsbury Town (above) are doing just that! They have all ten outfield players back by the edge of the box awaiting a Mike Pentecost free kick. The linesman is poised diligently looking for a marginal offside. A defensive Shrewsbury side managed to squeeze out a goalless draw at the Cottage in April 1971 against a jaded Fulham, but it was nevertheless one point nearer promotion for the home side.

Right: The club's photocall in August 1998 looks as though it's dragging on, with the players getting restless as the tracksuited and the suited fuss around. You can almost hear the players muttering, 'Come on, get on with it.'

Tyrone James makes his way into the officials entrance at Kenilworth Road in October 1975, before making his debut against Luton Town. A great deal was made of one of the earliest 'non-white' players to represent Fulham. He acquitted himself well and drew praise for his performance. On the day, the team were average and Luton was never one of our luckiest of grounds during this period. Despite conceding just the one goal we unfortunately didn't score any.

Below: If you can work out in which season this match took place, you are a real Fulham buff! Answer on last page.

FULHAM v. DARLINGTON
FOOTBALL LEAGUE, DIV. 2.

SUNDAY
PICTORIAL

FULHAM (2)

BEECHAM
1

DYER 2   BARRETT 3

OLIVER 4   McNAB (1) 5   WOLFE 6

HARRIS (1) 7   PROUSE 8   TONNER 9   CRAIG 10   PENN 11

Referee—Mr. G. N. WATSON.   Linesmen—Messrs. S. RICHARDSON and J. G. WORDLEY.

LITTLE 12   COCHRANE 13   RUDDY (1) 14   SCOTT 15   HOOPER 16

SLADE 17   ROBINSON 18   DICKSON 19

JOYCE 20   GREAVES 21

FAWCETT 22

DARLINGTON (1)

It's a hot day in August 1976, and it's the first Anglo-Scottish group stage match against the other team in SW6. Despite the empty stand, 12,000 have turned up to watch. Our intrepid photographer decides to frame the action with a group of snappers, and still manages to capture the ball in the picture as Alan Slough strikes one towards goal. Despite endeavour from both sides, it wasn't one for the purists and the match ended goalless. With just two draws in the three group games, Fulham failed to progress to the knock-out stage.

Below: John Beck (10) celebrates his goal against Bristol Rovers in November 1978. Chris Guthrie, at left in the picture, scored the other two goals in the 3–0 victory on a very foggy Friday evening. There were times when it wasn't possible to see one end of the pitch from the other, though in this picture Ken's camera has somewhat penetrated the gloom.

A good shot of Peter Mellor, Fulham's custodian for around four years. Signed for a bargain £20,000 from Burnley in January 1972, he provided a great deal of stability in an important position. After his signing, Fulham won and drew nine of their last thirteen games that season to ensure that survival was achieved when it had looked unlikely. He was an integral part of the team that took us to Wembley in 1975. Like most keepers he was prone to the odd gaffe, but his large physical presence proved to be a considerable deterrent to opposition forwards.

Here are five M's.

Clockwise from above:

Teddy Maybank
David Moreline
Richard Money
Terry Medwin
Bobby Moss.

A young Malcolm Macdonald signs autographs at Ayresome Park. One small fan appears to be edged out for the star's attention by a rather rude adult.

Riverside refreshment, sir? Cheers!

A cup final ticket, sir? These lovely gentlemen will oblige. They were assembled to assist in the distribution of tickets for the 1975 FA Cup final. On the wall behind them is a note mentioning programme vouchers. These were little triangles that had been printed in the programmes during the season that needed to be kept and then sent in to claim a ticket.

A collection from Stan Brown's picture album – pictures previously unseen. Many thanks to Stan's son, Darren, for these photographs.

At left Stan sits proudly in the middle of his school team.

After the relegation escape of 1966, Fulham took eighteen players on a close-season tour-cum-holiday in Asia, where they played local representative sides in exhibition matches. The other pictures here are from that tour. First Division Sheffield Wednesday also made the trip. The team had a number of social engagements and visited schools, training colleges and RAF units. They were well looked after and stayed at some point at the famous Raffles Hotel in Singapore. Pitches were hard, but made easier by the occasional welcome intervention of heavy rainfall. Fulham won four and drew one of six matches; Graham Leggat scored in every game, eleven goals in total. Manager Vic Buckingham summed up the tour: 'I would sincerely say that the Fulham flag flew high on the tour both on and off the field. The players brought only credit to their club, and deserve the utmost praise for their efforts.'

Overleaf: pages from one of Martin Plumb's scrapbooks. This was how we used to collect information before the days of the internet and on-line access.

LLOYD KEEPS UP CHASE

Mansfield 2 Fulham 3

A SUPERB 20-yard volley from Barry Lloyd last night hammered home the reminder that Fulham are still in with a promotion chance in Division Three.

Now they have gone 15 games without a beating and the possibility is that they could just get back to the Second. They are now eighth in the table.

Lloyd's winner was disputed by Mansfield as it whipped out from a stanchion, but after the referee consulted one of his linesmen it was allowed to stand.

LEVEL

Fulham had been a goal down after only a minute when Dai Jones ran on to score after being fouled near the half-way line.

They were two back in 27 minutes when Jones laid on another Mansfield cracker from Malcolm Partridge—his 14th goal of the season. That was the way it stayed until half-time.

Then, by the 51st minute, Fulham were level with goals from Jimmy Conway and striker Vic Halom.

They plundered both valuable points with Lloyd's goal—and were lucky when the referee waved play on after a Mansfield header from Dudley Roberts bounced down and away.

Fulham race to 15 not out

| Mansfield | .... | 2 | Fulham |

FULHAM, a goal down in a minute and two behind at the interval, came back with a tremendous second-half display at Mansfield to extend their unbeaten run to 15 games.

They levelled six minutes after half-time and went ahead after 69 minutes through Lloyd, whose fierce shot rebounded into play so hard that the goal was allowed only after the referee had consulted a linesman.

Mansfield strove desperately to equalise and only a fine save late on by Webster stopped Roberts doing so. Then loud appeals for a goal ignored after a Roberts header had rebounded off the bar on to the goal-line.

Mansfield's unbeaten home run of 13 games was ended, but they had only themselves to blame for failing to take more first-half chances.

DIVISION III

	P.	W.	D.	L.	F.	A.	
Orient	40	22	11	7	59	28	5
Bristol Rov	45	19	16	8	76	52	5
Brighton	44	22	9	13	54	40	5
Luton	41	19	13	9	70	42	5
Barnsley	44	18	14	12	64	58	5
Reading	42	20	10	12	76	70	5
Fulham	41	17	15	9	76	51	4
Mansfield	41	19	9	13	64	44	4

Mansfield took their ear lead through Jones. After son stimulating play by both sides two Fulham efforts were cleared the line—Partridge added Ma field's second (27 minutes).

Fulham's comeback was star by Conway after 47 minutes a Halom equalised four minutes la later.

Mansfield.—Brown; Pate, Walker, O ley, Boam, Waller, Partridge, McKen Jones, Roberts, Goodfellow. Sub. Sten

Fulham.—Webster; Pentecost, Ca ghan, Brown, Matthewson, Moreline, C way, Hallam, Earle, Lloyd, Barrett. S

Fulham make it early

FULHAM 2, BARROW 1

TWO QUICK goals at the beginning of each half got Fulham through. Yet, although they had most of the play, they were a little lucky to win.

When bottom-of-the-table Barrow did break they did it in style. Brown had to kick a Ledger shot off the line, and a Garbett banger bounced off the bar

Fulham's first goal was headed in by Richardson from a superb Haynes free-kick. The referee was about to whistle for a Fulham infringement when he glanced at his linesman, changed his mind, and gave the goal, in spite of Barrow protests.

Lloyd made it 2—0 with a gift goal, then quick thinking by Ellison brought Barrow back into the game with a hook shot

that beat Webster. Minutes later he hit the bar.

So Barrow nearly snatched a point from Fulham, whose strikers were right off form.

Brown, Barrett and Gilchrist can take credit for Fulham's win. Apart from them, Conway, in the second half, and Callaghan no one impressed. Webster was mediocre. Tranter poor and Haynes patchy.

The game ended on a typical Fulham note with Haynes and Callaghan missing chances.

FULHAM: Webster 5; Gilchrist 7, Matthewson 5, Callaghan 6, *BROWN 5, Tranter 4, Haynes 6; Conway 6, Richardson (inj.) 6, Earle 6, Barrett 7. Sub.: Lloyd 6.

BARROW: Heyes 6; Dean 5, Knoble 5, Arrowsmith 7, Cooper 5; Morrin 6, Hartland 5, *ELLISON 8; Garbett 7, Ledger 5, Mulvaney 5.

Referee: M. Kerkhof (Oxford) 5.

RALPH HADLEY

STEVE EARLE
Fulham

JOHNNY HAYNES RECALLS

JOHNNY HAYNES, who completed 600 senior appearances for Fulham last month, recalls some of the highlights of his almost legendary career.

His League debut—"Boxing day 1952 against Southampton."

The first of his 56 England caps—"I scored on my debut against Ireland in Belfast in 1954."

His greatest match—"When I captained England to a 9-3 victory over Scotland at Wembley in 1961."

His greatest player — "Undoubtedly Tom Finney."

His biggest disappointments

—"Two F.A. Cup semi-final defeats, against Manchester United in 1958 and Burnley in 1962, both after replays."

And his immediate ambition —"To help lift Fulham from the foot of the Second Division."

With the Craven Cottage club currently languishing at rock bottom in the Second Division, Haynes is going to have his work cut out. However, he has led the famous London escapologists to safety many times before and is confident that he can do it again.

LES BARRETT (Fulham)

LHAM held a shock 3—0 half-
e lead at Reading.

gift goal scored by
RRETT gave Fulham a
enth-minute lead. A mistake
Dixon let in Barrett, who hit
ow drive from close range.

olice moved in to the crowd
minutes before the start to
ak up a fight. Several youths
e escorted from the ground.

FULHAM were two up after
minutes from another defen-
e blunder. Sharpe put a
arance to Conway, whose
cross was slipped into an
pty goal by HALOM.

EARLE scored in the 36th
nute with a clever side flick
nr a cross by Barrett.

lf-time: Reading 0, Fulham 3.
Reading hit back strongly on
restart, but their failings in
ence were exploited by the
k Fulham attack.

Reading's prolific scoring
wards were tightly held by a
rce-tackling Fulham defence
d Webster was rarely troubled.

LES BARRETT . . . Fulham's
Young England forward.

Fulham v. Leeds—17.9.66. *Bremner (No. 4) being tripped by Clarke of Fulham.*

Halom is happy at Craven Cottage

VIC HALOM, Fulham's £35,000 signing from Orient, had his first game against Portsmouth on Saturday. It was no dream debut . . . but that doesn't worry Vic. He said: "It's always nice to get a goal in your first game, but I'm not worried that I didn't this time. It takes time to settle with a new team."

Halom has a big responsibility at Fulham. Manager Bobby Robson is pinning a lot of his hopes for a revival on the scoring flair of a player who was a wing-half until 12 months ago.

That was when Orient signed him for £3,000, and he soon proved himself worth every penny—as a striker. He says: "Switching to the forward line was the best move I ever made. I was a bit worried, but it came off."

Halom had scored eight times in 11 games before he joined Fulham, who beat Derby for the signature by just five minutes.

Would he have gone to Derby if manager Brian Clough had arrived a bit earlier? Said Halom: "I'm happy to be at Fulham. They're a good club."

GEORGE COHEN

New hopes
GEORGE COHEN

. . continues his uphill struggle to get fit. Out of hospital but on crutches after his second knee operation, the Fulham right-back says: "I hope to be playing in November." That's something we all hope—the game can ill-afford to be without players of George's class and intelligence.

Pay dispute
JOHN RICHARDSON

. . is the latest player in dispute with a London club. The 19-year-old Brentford wing-half wants more than a basic £20 a week and is taking his case to arbitration. If that's not satisfactory, Richardson will ask to be listed. Several First Division clubs are watching the case of Richardson, who is a nephew of Billy Gray, the Notts County manager.

3 GOALS IN 3 MINS.—THEN FULHAM TRAIL

BRISTOL R. 3, FULHAM 2.

Three goals in three minutes . . . Fulham 2—1 up then 3—2 down . . . that was the siuation in their game against Bristol Rovers at Eastville today.

They took the lead through CONWAY in the 23rd-minute after a clever move between the scorer and Barrett. Within a minute, however, Rovers had equalised with a penalty by JARMAN after he had been brought down by Brown.

The action wasn't over, though, for almost from the kick-off Fulham went into the lead again with a splendid solo goal from EARLE.

Jarman's goal set a club scoring record for a winger. It was his 111th goal—and 400th game—for Rovers.

Half-time: Bristol R. 1, Fulham 2.

Fulham, seeking their first away win of the season, went close to increasing their lead when Barrett hit the bar.

Instead, Rovers equalised three minutes after half-time when STUBBS scored after a bad back pass by Gilchrist.

Rovers took the lead for the first time when a mis-timed kick from GRAYDON went in off the post.

The only ever visit to Southport by the Cottagers was in April 1970. A gas holder and a sparse crowd of just over 3,000 overlook Vic Halom as, watched by Mike Pentecost, he gets in a right-wing cross early on in the match. Fulham continue to bombard the Southport goal, and the picture below shows Fred Callaghan firing in a 20-yarder through a posse of defenders.

Below: our first-half goal at Southport. As the twilight deepens, Les Barrett pounces with a downward header between goalkeeper and post.

Another picture from the match at Southport featured opposite. By now dusk has arrived and the floodlights are on. A shot from Jimmy Conway flashes past the post, and Ken's camera catches the Southport goalkeeper bathed in a halo of light. Conway has the last laugh as he scores in the second half to secure Fulham's 2–0 win.

No luck. Johnny Haynes, through on goal, is thwarted by a great sliding tackle from, who else, ex-Fulham man Alan Mullery. At a packed White Hart Lane in February 1966, a Fulham team that was finally beginning to gel, find themselves 0–3 down after just fifteen minutes. But then in a remarkable seven-minute spell Fulham score three goals – and hit the post! Fulham are finally undone by Cliff Jones (who nearly always scored against the Cottagers) completing a hat trick with a clearly offside goal, the referee over-ruling a flagging linesman. Seven goals before half time, pretty rare indeed. There were no goals in the second half, but having lost by that bizarre 3–4 score, Fulham find their luck turns the following week with a famous victory against champions elect Liverpool.

In September 1980 Fulham visit Fratton Park, and chairman Ernie Clay takes the opportunity to promote Fulham's cause with TV commentator Tony Gubba. Gubba was one of the most respected journalists around and had a career in broadcasting that spanned over forty years. He sadly passed away aged just 69.

Below: action from the match. O'Driscoll, Lock and Wilson are all in the picture but no-one seems to be making much contact. On the right is Pompey's former Orient midfielder Terry Brisley. On this day, the visitors slide to a 0–1 defeat. In seven matches around this time, Fulham suffered that identical result four times, but picked up in mid-season to finish in mid-table.

Season 1995–96 beckons and these are tough times indeed for Fulham FC – in the bottom league and their status as a club still under a cloud. However, the spirit and humour that epitomises our team still manages to shine through those dark days. In the pre-season photoshoot manager Ian Branfoot has managed to dispel the gloom and a happy squad prepares to smile for the camera.

On the far right of the players, Micky Adams appears to be detached from the merriment, possibly pondering over his future role at the club. But no-one can deny the steadying and solid influence that Branfoot brought to the club at a time when it really needed it.

Below: Referee Clive Thomas does what he likes doing best. Out comes the yellow card for one or more of the Millwall defenders having to line up in the goal area, to face a Fulham free kick at the old Den in January 1981. It wasn't a good day for the Whites either, as an early Davies goal was cancelled out by three Millwall goals from defensive errors.

Stan Brown's super, 22-carat, diamond-studded, gilt-edged goal – as described in the programme – has been seen before, but is still worthy of inclusion here. The goal gives Fulham a deserved equaliser against First Division FA Cup holders West Bromwich Albion in February 1969 in the fourth round.

Below: delight for Jim Conway and Steve Earle too, as Stan acknowledges the goal and the crowd. There seems to be an inquest being held by centre half John Talbut (pointing) with Doug Fraser as to who should have been marking Stan. Erm, we think it was you, John!

Albion finally scraped through 2–1 with a scruffy goal in the closing stages but Fulham, struggling in the Second Division, proved that on their day they were a match for anyone.

At the start of season 2000–01, Fulham won the first eleven matches. Pictured here is a goal in the tenth match, a 2–1 victory at home to Blackburn Rovers in October; Barry Hayles watches as Fabrice Fernandes' shot flies into the net.

Below: a real archive picture from supporter Maureen Grimwood, showing a youth squad from 1961–62. Back row, from left: Martin Townsend, unknown, Rodney Marsh, Mike Jones, unknown, unknown. Middle row: George Milton (coach), Mike Doyle, Mike Brown, Bobby Downes, Roger Durdle, Brian Nichols, John Hayes, Eric Symons. Front row: Tom McCloud, Ignatious McKenzie, Fred Callaghan, Tony Goodgame, Steve Earle. The three unknowns in the back row are probably Gowland, Sheehan and Borst, but possibly not in that sequence.

Rodney Marsh, Brian Nichols, Fred Callaghan and Steve Earle all made the Fulham first team; Tony Goodgame went on to play for Orient; Martin Townsend also played two games in goal for Fulham; and forward Mike Brown played four games for Fulham and over 100 league games for Millwall, Luton Town and Colchester United. Probably the most successful was defender Mike Jones who went on to play almost 300 league games for Leyton Orient and Charlton Athletic.

This is the first leg of the Anglo-Scottish Cup final in 1975 at Ayresome Park. Defender Ernie Howe is up with the forwards trying to break the deadlock against Middlesbrough's watertight defence, but we are outnumbered by six to two. Les Strong's own goal decided this first-leg tie. The second leg was equally dour and tight and produced little football and no goals, despite Fulham giving it all they had against their First Division opponents. Some considered that the one goal that decided the final was the only shot on target in 180 minutes. Middlesbrough were well drilled and organised at the back by Jack Charlton, reliant on getting men behind the ball and scoring in breakaways. The year they won this trophy, they conceded just eleven league goals at home all season, a better record than league champions Liverpool!

Below: Fulham manager Alec Stock watches as Jack Charlton congratulates his players on their triumph. Magnanimous in defeat as always, a smiling Stock remains in the background and allows his victorious opponents their moment. As Bobby Robson used to say when your own team was defeated, 'Think of the joy in the other dressing room.'

A couple of pictures from Jon Hall, a noted recorder of the passing scene. Above: Fulham faithful somewhere in a foreign field hail a winning team. Below: Hull City's first ever match in the top flight was at home to the Whites. Ever the generous ones, we contrived to let Hull win by 2 goals to 1. Pictured below is a header from Simon Davies that came to nought.

Posing in front of a crowd well into double figures are players representing David Lloyd's fanzine 'There's Only One F In Fulham' and the Fulham programme department, about to do battle in a challenge match on the famous turf in 1999. (We regret that some names escape us. Also, this picture has been scanned from a small print from an old Instamatic camera, so it's a little indistinct. Thanks to Kevin O'Callaghan for digging the print from out of his loft.)

Back row: Patrick Mascall, unknown, Gary Mulcahey, unknown, Frank Boahene, Reverend Gary Piper, Kevin O'Callaghan, Michael Heatley, Ross unknown, Bob Cain, Anthony Hough.

Front row: Neil Rodford, unknown, David Hamilton, Pudsey, Nobby unknown, Mike Jones, Javier Garcia.

VIVA EL FULHAM

(TO THE TUNE OF Y VIVA ESPANA, New Lyrics by Eddie Seago)

BY THE COTTAGERS

Recorded on Sonet Records SON 2059

(Sonet Records are sold in all good record shops - dist. by Pye)

SING LOUD TO THE TUNE OF Y VIVA ESPANA

'VIVA EL FULHAM'

Down the Fulham Road we're burning with ambition
The first division is where we wanna be
And if you've seen what a team we've got this season
You know the reason we'll get there easily
But first we're heading down the Wembley way
To show the world that we can really play.

CHORUS

OH THIS YEAR WE'RE GONNA WIN THE CUP...HEY VIVA EL FULHAM
THEN NEXT YEAR YOU KNOW WE'RE GOING UP...HEY VIVA EL FULHAM
ALAN M. IS A WONDER THAT'S FOR SURE...HEY VIVA EL FULHAM
AND BOBBY - WELL DO WE NEED SAY MORE! ...IT'S FULHAM POR FAVOR

Tommy Trinder used to hide behind his trilby
But soon he will be the proudest in the land
He'll be thinking of his cottage by the river
When we deliver that scoreline in his hand
And there behind us steady as a rock
That softly spoken tiger Alec Stock.

CHORUS OH THIS YEAR WE'RE GONNA WIN THE CUP...etc.

There's a way to penetrate those packed defences
Attack 'em senseless then pass the ball to Viv
'Cos from Ian there in goal to Les and Jimmy
We'll all be giving as much as we can give
We're gonna keep on scoring golden goals
It keeps the guvnor off the old King Cole.

All together now! It's the cup final song...

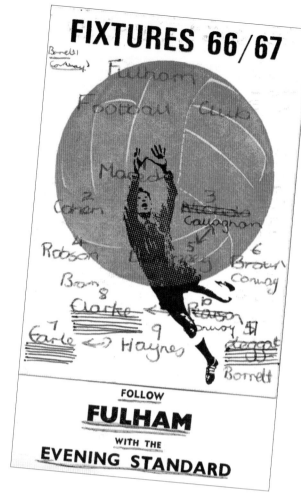

FOLLOW

FULHAM

WITH THE

EVENING STANDARD

Below: Peter Woodman is very proud of this junior Supporters' Club card from over 50 years ago.

Bottom: We had forgotten, but it seems that autograph sheets (with original signatures, not copies) were on sale in the club shop. What's also amazing about this sheet is that virtually all the signatures are very readable!

Peter Kitchen soars above former Fulham centre half Paul Went to try and get a header on target during the match against Peter's former club Orient in April 1979. He's watched by Henry Hughton of Orient, Tony Gale, and former Spurs man Ian Moores (who scored that day). An entertaining game finished 2–2 but Kitchen was out of luck, pretty much as usual. It took a Kevin Lock penalty three minutes from the end to salvage a point for the home side. Orient's other goal came from the beautifully named Tunji Banjo.

A run of 15 home wins (imagine that!) came to an end in April 1999 when Wrexham visited the Cottage. Fulham were already champions of Division Two under Kevin Keegan, but a dour Welsh side managed to keep the Cottagers to a 1–1 draw. This was our goal, headed in by Paul Peschisolido.

Below: another gem from one of our supporters, Maureen Grimwood. This is the entire Fulham first team (Barry Mealand in for George Cohen) taking part in a prize-giving and reception for the West Fulham Sunday League at Hammersmith Town Hall in 1963.

Season 1968–69 saw Johnny Haynes honoured for his 19 years of loyal service to the club. He was presented with the traditional gold watch by chairman Tommy Trinder – and, dear readers, we have tracked down that very watch. It was acquired by supporter Peter Heffernan, who now runs an Irish sports bar (whatever that is…) in Manchester. Peter was kind enough to send us these pictures of the watch, still in excellent condition and still with its Asprey's box. The inscription calls Haynes 'the club's greatest player ever'. Still no argument with that!

"Haynes will either be fit for Saturday or he won't be — now what about washing up?"

Testimonial Boxing-Dinner to Johnny the ONE

All this despite Tommy Trinder's help!

* ONE OF OUR TRULY GREAT INTERNATIONALS.
* FIRST £100 PER WEEK PLAYER.
* ONE CLUB ONLY MAN

CONNAUGHT ROOMS. 16th SEPTEMBER 1968.

Aerial action from Allan Clarke, watched by Steve Earle, against already relegated Blackpool in April 1967.

Below: Erudite Fulham fan Peter Thomson waylays Simon Morgan during training, to impart a few tips on improving the team's performance. One of his suggestions may have been for Simon to take more exercise.

The other picture shows a riverside view of Craven Cottage. Mr Morgan denies all knowledge of the bicycle wheel deposited in the trees, but there are reports that Mr Thomson had to walk home.

FOOTBALL
AT
CRAVEN COTTAGE

Monday, 8th January   3rd Rnd. F.A. Youth Cup   K.O. 7 pm

CHARLTON

Saturday, 13th January   Football Combination   K.O. 2-15 p.m.

NORWICH CITY

Saturday, 20th January   Football League   K.O. 3-0 p.m.

LEICESTER CITY

Saturday, 27th January   Football Combination   K.O. 2-15 p.m.

OXFORD UNITED

Monday, 29th January   Football Combination   K.O. 7-0 p.m.

CRYSTAL PALACE

Saturday, 3rd February   Football Combination   K.O. 2-15 p.m.

OXFORD UNITED

League Prices :   GROUND 4/-   BOYS 2/-   ENCLOSURE 5/-

STAND SEATS 8/-, 10/-, 15/-

Combination Prices :   GROUND 2/-   BOYS 1/-   STANDS EXTRA

CENTRAL PRINTING CO. (CHAS. SOWDEN) LTD., BURNLEY LANCS.

1968

Bobby Campbell's squad in 1978. Back row: Ian Salter (youth team coach), Ron Woolnough (physio), Tony Mahoney, Steve Hatter, Tony Gale, Gerry Peyton, Perry Digweed, Geoff Banton, Kevin Lock, John Margerrison, Mike Kelly (coach); front row: Gordon Boyd, John Evanson, Terry Bullivant, Bobby Campbell (manager), Brian Greenaway, Richard Money, Les Strong, Gordon Davies.

Still remembered as a wonder goal is Jon Harley's strike that gave us a 2–1 victory over Aston Villa at our temporary Loftus Road home in February 2003. Jon is at top left in the picture above and has just fired on goal from well over 30 yards. It all happened too fast for our cameraman – the ball has long gone out of the frame. It all happened too fast for the Villa goalkeeper as well (below); he never saw it coming either.

A celebratory evening for the rugby club in the early 1980s. Rugby captain Reg Bowden tells it how it is to Fulham historian Dennis Turner and club secretary George Noyce.

And yet another celebratory evening, where Tony Gale, Terry Mancini and Ron Woolnough seem to be enjoying the occasion.

Geoff Horsfield receives a player of the month award; former referee Jack Taylor holds the bottle.

Below: Famous fan Alex Ferguson ('The Traveller', not the other, less famous, Ferguson) holds forth during a Cottagers' away match somewhere in Europe.

Right: Staying up.

FOOTBALL ASSOCIATION CHALLENGE CUP COMPETITION

FINAL

FULHAM
VERSUS
WEST HAM UNITED

SATURDAY, 3rd MAY, 1975   Kick-off 3 p.m.

Official Souvenir Programme . . . 20p.

EMPIRE WEMBLEY STADIUM

Putney Cricket Club
Founded 1870
(Affiliated to The Club Cricket Conference)
(Member of the Surrey Association of Cricket Clubs)
President—SIR HUGH LINSTEAD, O.B.E., M.P.

The Chairman's Match in aid of the New Cricket Pavilion Fund

PUTNEY C.C. v. FULHAM F.C.

The Putney Lower Common Ground
AUGUST BANK HOLIDAY, 3rd AUGUST, 1964

FULHAM F.C.
†1. J. Haynes ....
2. B. Jezzard ....
*3. A. Stevens ....
4. T. Macedo ....
5. J. Langley ....
6. R. Robson ....
7. G. Leggatt ....
8. B. O'Connell ....
9. M. Cooke ....
10. R. Stratton ....
11. R. Marsh ....
12. B. Howfield ....
Fall of Wickets: 1- 2- 3- 4- 5- 6- 7- 8- 9- 10- 11-

PUTNEY C.C.
1. J. Kelvin ....
2. P. Thorn ....
†3. M. Lickens ....
4. E. Sellwood ....
5. D. Jordan ....
6. E. Pilgrim ....
7. P. Barton

A treasured signed cup final programme from John Stubbs.

Right: two items from Fulham fan David Tachon. The annual pre-season match against Putney Cricket Club, that year in aid of the Pavilion Fund, continued for many years. Note that in 1964 this was played on the August Bank Holiday Monday which was then the FIRST Monday of the month; there was always pressure to move it to the end of the month which eventually happened, but in Scotland it is still the first Monday. Fulham's team contains manager Bedford Jezzard with coach Arthur Stevens as wicketkeeper at a sprightly 43 years old. Johnny Haynes was of course captain.

Black and Lowe should really be the name of a firm that offers counselling for depression, but the two ex-Fulham internationals ran a sports equipment shop and business for many years in Tolworth Surrey, a couple of miles from Motspur Park. Goalkeeper Ian Black is pictured on the left, and Eddie Lowe is in the picture below.

In March 1962, after losing eleven league games in a row, we secured a draw with Nottingham Forest, before playing Sheffield United. An on-song Fulham won easily 5–2. Reg Matthewson made his debut that day for Sheffield United and our centre forward Maurice Cook gave him a torrid time, scoring a hat trick. The picture shows an even rarer event – a goal for Eddie Lowe (6), which he volleys in with aplomb past the diving keeper. Lowe scored just ten goals in his 511 games, so pictures like this are gold dust! For him this was a purple patch as he scored three in two months between January and March 1962.

Rob Scott shows style at Lincoln, with hardly a hair out of place.

Left: a television grab shot of two controversial characters from Fulham's recent past: Bobby Zamora and Martin Jol.

Opposite: *Photographer Ken has captured many famous players in Fulham colours, but this picture is a real gem.*

Here's World Cup winning captain Bobby Moore posing in Fulham's away strip and smiling for Ken's camera.

This is Rodney McAree, forever remembered as the man who put the ball in the Carlisle net. Fulham fans will know that the victory at Brunton Park in April 1997 was a major springboard in our rise to the Premiership. Thanks, Rodney!

Right: The 1951–52 official yearbook featured on the cover an illustration used for years as the cover of the programme.

Below: Andy Sayer signs for fans at an unidentified ground. Andy signed for Fulham in August 1988 and started to score freely. However, the goals began to dry up at a difficult time for the club, and within a season and a half he had left.

For the man of taste and style we offer these cuff links, exclusive to the Supporters' Club.

Roger Cross is pictured here a few minutes after the start at Swindon's County Ground in his second game for Fulham. He had been bought to bolster a shot-shy attack after the departure of Vic Halom in September 1971. In this match Fulham played well for twenty minutes, but after Swindon scored their first goal, Fulham's confidence waned. The Whites eventually lost 0–4 and, worryingly at the time, it was their seventh consecutive game without a goal.

Below: Skipper Barry Lloyd, goalkeeper Malcolm Webster and new signing Roger Cross pose with three of the team that are promoting 'Lucky Strike somethings' in 1971. We were baffled as we didn't think Fulham would have been promoting Lucky Strike cigarettes, the T-Shirts seeming to imply Lucky Strike Mints. And indeed the internet rescued us as we now know that Lucky Strike Mints were launched that year. Apparently they were printed with the names of football teams and were promoted as a way of doing the pools. They were produced by Matlows responsible for such confectionery as Lovehearts and Refreshers.

Jimmy Conway rises high in the Sheffield Wednesday penalty area, but can't quite direct his header on goal during the match in February 1975. We won the match 2–1, with goals from Les Barrett and Alan Mullery.

Below: Keeper Ted Hinton safely gathers the ball at a snowbound Cottage in the late 1940s.

Below right: Fans help clear the pitch before the match against Gillingham in December 1970. The match had been moved from Boxing Day to the 28th, to avoid a clash with Chelsea. The match had further been moved from evening to afternoon. At kick-off, piles of snow sat on the cinder track around the pitch, which was very muddy. The match would not have gone ahead today. It proved a bit of a Christmas pantomime farce; players slid and fell all over the place, whilst valiantly trying to provide some sort of entertainment. In the circumstances Fulham were relieved to secure a 1–0 win over bottom-placed Gillingham, via Vic Halom's first goal for three months.

Against Wolves in December 1961, Fulham goalkeeper Tony Macedo injures his shoulder making a flying save. He then plays on the wing (this was before the days of substitutes) and full back Jimmy Langley takes over between the sticks. Both players do extremely well, and Fulham look like securing a well-earned point until the visitors net the only goal in the dying moments of the game. Here gentleman Jim punches clear from a Wolves attack.

Our thanks to June Gilbert for the picture.

Two very important people from Fulham's history. Owner Mohamed Al Fayed endeared himself to the Fulham faithful with his dedication to the cause and propelling the club into the Premiership.

And Johnny Haynes, well, need we say more!

Secretary Graham Hortop shows prospective season ticket buyers in the 1970s the many delights of the new Riverside Stand.

Right: An interior designer is pleased to demonstrate how the wallpaper for the new stand will enhance the customer experience.

In December 1980 we played out a 2–2 draw against Huddersfield, both our goals being scored by Gordon Davies. His first came after just 45 seconds; his second is pictured above. His glancing header from a swirling left-wing cross easily beats the Terriers' keeper – but Gordon does look as though he may have been offside. Still, the linesman was up with the play – and no flag.

Below: chaos in the Bristol Rovers goal area at Eastville in January 1976, but no joy as Fulham slide to a 0–1 defeat.

This picture, of a flying Dean Coney against Wimbledon in the 4–1 victory in February 1982, was originally going to be the picture on the front cover of this scrapbook. However, after much heated editorial discussion and cooled Petit Chablis, it was Gordon Davies who got the final vote.

Opposite page: *Bill Taylor was one of those quiet lovely men – and an immensely talented coach. After being a fringe player (his own term) for three league clubs, he was appointed by Bill Dodgin as reserve and junior coach in August 1971. Upon Alec Stock's appointment as manager, he became first-team coach, and was pivotal in Fulham's improved form and run to the FA Cup final in 1975. He went on to coach First Division Manchester City, and was later appointed by England manager Ron Greenwood (formerly a player with Fulham) as the first Scotsman ever to coach England. At the peak of his career he was diagnosed with cancer and sadly died at the early age of just 42. His position in Fulham folklore is firmly established.*

Next page: *another flying Fulham forward – this time Chris Guthrie.*

Gordon Davies spots himself at the Black And White Years exhibition of Fulham photographs in 2003.

Below: a through-the-net view of manager Bobby Campbell walking off with Luton's Harry Haslam at the end of the match in February 1977. Both look glum, but Haslam was the marginally happier, his team having secured a 2–1 victory. Haslam had been assistant to manager Bobby Robson at Fulham in 1968.

   Below right: a signed picture of Robin Lawler, a stalwart defender throughout the Fifties.

It's the very first game of 1978, and a cold and miserable afternoon. Fulham are playing their fourth league game in eight days (ah, those were the days when men were men!). The derby at the Valley is at a stalemate; the Whites are the better team but cannot score. Our caption writer is listening on the wireless, and then the LBC commentator reports: 'There's been a late goal at Charlton...' His heart sinks (you know that feeling), but this time it's good news. John Mitchell's late shot has been pushed on to the post by the goalkeeper and it rebounds to a defender whose back pass to the keeper is hesitant and short – and in nips Brian Greenaway at 100mph to slot home the loose ball. 1–0 and a deserved victory.

OH, WHAT A CARRY ON AT THE PALACE!

THE REFEREE whose watch stopped caused a sensation at Selhurst Park. Players who had kicked off their boots and were head-

We had some decent and feisty encounters with Crystal Palace in the Seventies. Many were eventful, but none more so than our visit to Selhurst Park in October 1978. The pictures above show Brian Greenaway taking a pass from Richard Money, outpacing centre half Jim Cannon and firing a low shot under Palace goalkeeper Burridge in off the post for the only goal of the game.

The bizarre part was the referee (E Hughes) blowing for full time five minutes early, producing a match of 85 minutes. The teams walked off, some players were apparently already in the bath. Many supporters had left the ground, some were in cars suddenly hearing on radio's Sports Report 'result not yet in'. News quickly spread, but many thought it was just a hoax or joke – it wasn't. Some went back to the ground, most didn't. The referee alerted by his linesmen requested that the teams return to the field to play out the five minutes, plus injury time. Somehow Fulham survived that hectic period to secure the victory and even managed to have a second goal disallowed.

Photographer Coton's view of the disallowed goal is shown right. He was in his car at the time, having a cup of tea...

Gordon Davies sits this one out...

A snap of a television broadcast in March 1976 when Eamonn Andrews waylaid Alan Mullery at the Cottage to utter those famous words: 'This is your life!'.

Alan's testimonial was held at this time, and he is pictured left at a presentation from director Chappie D'Amato and manager Alec Stock.

At right, Sir Alf Ramsey, alongside Bobby Moore, team captain at the testimonial evening, introduces his Old England side to play an Ex-Fulham team in a curtain-raiser to the main match, Scotland versus the Rest of Great Britain.

Below: From that main match Jimmy Greaves (of Brentwood) scores against Bob Wilson, one of many highlights in a great evening.

Stars and stripes. Above: Fulham field a star-studded side with quite a few first-teamers against amateurs Kingstonian in the London Challenge Cup match in October 1965. The Whites were 0–2 down with just a few minutes remaining, but then Marsh struck with two goals in four minutes. His first goal, pictured here, came at the end of a fine solo run. We lost the replay!

Below: a League Cup replay in October 1964 against Reading, then of the Third Division. First Division Fulham had been drawn away in the tie and a partisan crowd had seen Maurice Cook (who would join Reading the following season) score the goal that enabled Fulham to cling on to a 1–1 draw. The replay should have been a formality and only 5,000 turn up at Craven Cottage. But this is Fulham, and Reading have other ideas. They deservedly win 3–1 and our only goal comes from a powerful long-range drive from Bobby Robson (not in the picture) that is in the net before the goalkeeper can move.

ANSWERS

Pages 40 and 41. Players are named from left to right, row by row.

Page 40: first row: *Chris Guthrie, Malcolm Webster, Ray Evans, Bill Dodgin;*
row 2: *Peter Kitchen, Joe Stapleton, Peter Marinello, Mark Pearson, Ian Seymour, Paul Went;*
row 3: *Alan Warboys, John Gilchrist, Jackie Henderson, George Johnston, George Best, Brian Nichols;*
row 4: *Ernie Howe, Gary Peters, Rodney Marsh, Jimmy Hill, Terry Parmenter, Reg Stratton;*
row 5: *Ray Houghton, John Ryan, Stan Horne, Dave Clement, John Margerrison, Allan Clarke;*
row 6: *Ronnie Goodlass, John Fraser, Teddy Maybank, Vic Halom, Dai Edwards, Derek Lampe.*

Page 41: first row: *Roy Bentley, Cliff Jones, Terry Dyson;*
row 2: *John Dowie, Jack McClelland, Tosh Chamberlain, Dean Coney, Jeff Hopkins, Dave Metchick;*
row 3: *Dale Tempest, John Evanson, Bobby Howfield, Brian Greenaway, John Richardson, Jim Stannard;*
row 4: *Dave Roberts, Frank Large, Paul Parker, Robin Lawler, Geoff Banton, John Conway;*
row 5: *Roger Cross, John Doherty, Wilf Tranter, Mike Pentecost, Peter O'Sullivan, Ken Hewkins;*
row 6: *Joe Gilroy, Barry Mealand, Dave Moreline, Steve Hatter, Tony Mahoney, Mike Johnson.*

Page 58: *The grounds that Fulham visited are, clockwise from top left: Chester, Orient, Carlisle, Luton, Mansfield, Macclesfield, Stoke, Southampton and Northampton.*

Page 97: *The programme was for the match in September 1926.*

ASHWATER
PRESS